The Word in Other Words

Cycle A Sermons for
Pentecost Sunday Through
Proper 14
Based on the Gospel Texts

Rev. Dr. Tom M. Garrison

CSS Publishing Company, Inc.
Lima, Ohio

THE WORD IN OTHER WORDS

FIRST EDITION
Copyright © 2013
by CSS Publishing Co., Inc.

Published by CSS Publishing Company, Inc., Lima, Ohio 45807. All rights reserved. No part of this publication may be reproduced in any manner whatsoever without the prior permission of the publisher, except in the case of brief quotations embodied in critical articles and reviews. Inquiries should be addressed to: CSS Publishing Company, Inc., Permissions Department, 5450 N. Dixie Highway, Lima, Ohio 45807.

Scripture quotations are from the New Revised Standard Version of the Bible. Copyright 1989 by the Division of Christian Education of the National Council of the Churches of Christ in the USA. Used by permission.

Library of Congress Cataloging-in-Publication Data

Garrison, Tom.
 The Word in other words : Cycle A sermons for Pentecost Sunday through proper 14 based on the gospel texts / Rev. Dr. Tom Garrison. -- First edition.
   pages cm.
 Includes bibliographical references and index.
 ISBN 0-7880-2767-0 (alk. paper)
 1. Bible. Matthew--Sermons. 2. Pentecost season--Sermons. 3. Common lectionary (1992) I. Title.

BS2575.54.G37 2013
252'.64--dc23

2013028287

For more information about CSS Publishing Company resources, visit our website at www.csspub.com, email us at csr@csspub.com, or call (800) 241-4056.

ISBN-13: 978-0-7880-2767-3
ISBN-10: 0-7880-2767-0

PRINTED IN USA

Renata
The person I can always speak to openly, trust completely, and know will bring out the best in me.

Acknowledgments

Pegge Phillips
for her typing, support, and encouragement

Pensacola Beach Church (UCC)
for accepting my ministry and sharing their love

Linda Garrison Brown
my sister who always encourages my efforts

Table of Contents

Pentecost Sunday   7
    Despair, Hope, Easter, and Pentecost
    John 20:19-23

Holy Trinity Sunday   15
    As You Go, Remember…
    Matthew 28:16-20

Proper 7   21
Pentecost 2
Ordinary Time 12
    Death, Risk, and Confidence
    Matthew 10:24-39

Proper 8   29
Pentecost 3
Ordinary Time 13
    Jesus Morality
    Matthew 10:40-42

Proper 9   35
Pentecost 4
Ordinary Time 14
    What Do You Bring to the Table?
    Matthew 11:16-19, 25-30

Proper 10   41
Pentecost 5
Ordinary Time 15
    Playing One Hand
    Matthew 13:1-9, 18-23

Proper 11   49
Pentecost 6
Ordinary Time 16
    What You Don't Know Can Hurt You
    Matthew 13:24-30, 36-43

Proper 12   57
Pentecost 7
Ordinary Time 17
    Face-to-Face With the Kingdom
    Matthew 13:31-33, 44-52

Proper 13   65
Pentecost 8
Ordinary Time 18
    Gratitude and Coping
    Matthew 14:13-21

Proper 14   75
Pentecost 9
Ordinary Time 19
    Giving and Receiving
    Matthew 14:22-33

If You Like This Book...   83

Pentecost Sunday
John 20:19-23

Despair, Hope, Easter, and Pentecost

> When it was evening on that day, the first day of the week, and the doors of the house where the disciples had met were locked for fear of the Jews, Jesus came and stood among them and said, "Peace be with you." After he said this, he showed them his hands and his side. Then the disciples rejoiced when they saw the Lord. Jesus said to them again, "Peace be with you. As the Father has sent me, so I send you." When he had said this, he breathed on them and said to them, "Receive the Holy Spirit. If you forgive the sins of any, they are forgiven them; if you retain the sins of any, they are retained."

In an old poem titled "The Widow in the Bye Street," John Masefield depicts a scene of dramatic agony. A young man is about to be executed for crimes against the state, and in the crowd that is gathered to witness this event stands his widowed mother, who is about to be left all alone in the world. When the trapdoor opens and the rope has finished its work, this pathetic soul crumples to the ground and begins to sob uncontrollably, and those nearby hear her say something about "broken things, too broke to mend." Part of this anguish has to do with the past and her sense of failure as a parent, which is now being made visible for all to see. But an even greater part of that anguish has to do with the future and the utter sense of hopelessness that is now closing in upon her. It is an awful thing to feel that your very existence is not just broken, but broken beyond repair. That phrase "too broke to mend" is an awesome one, for it suggests there is no future, nothing left to live for, no sense of promise or possibility out ahead to beckon you forward. As I understand it, this is the functional essence of despair. It is to find yourself at a certain juncture in life where there is a past and a present but no future — nothing at all out ahead to look forward to. This has to be one of life's most devastating experiences, and yet such moments come to us all in relation to our health, our marriages, our children, or our careers.

John Claypool, the late Episcopal priest, who at the time was a Baptist preacher, said he found himself at such a dead-end when death claimed his little daughter on a snowy January night. She died of leukemia, and he said for a while everything within and around him seemed to die. He said there were a million memories and all kinds of immediate pressures, but the problem was there did not seem to be any kind of future left. That which had made life so meaningful was now broken, apparently "too broke to mend."

There have been so many others who have, do, and will experience this same sort of anguish. Not long ago I was in a cardiac care unit beside the bed of a man who was just regaining consciousness after a crippling heart attack. He asked if I had heard about what had happened to him, and when I nodded, he said anxiously: "What's left for me, Preacher? What do I do now that my body is broken and my career is over?" It is the first question that always comes to mind when the bottom drops out and the way things used to be is no more. What about tomorrow? Do I even have one? These are the questions I dare say most adults have asked at one time or another, and for that reason we would do well to ponder again the Easter story, for this is what it is all about — despair, the problem of the future, the agony of broken things that seem too broke to mend. There is a word here that can change our whole outlook if we will let it.

It is interesting to note the parallel between Masefield's poem and the first Easter. Here too is the story of a young man being executed by the state in the presence of his mother. And when he died that Friday afternoon around three o'clock, more expired than just a human body. The hopes of literally hundreds of people were shattered by this demise, for they had thought this one to be the Messiah. From the day he first appeared in Galilee, preaching the good news of the kingdom and doing acts of power, the word had spread that Israel's long-awaited deliverer had arrived, and the common people began to stir with excitement. Then just as swiftly as his fortunes had risen, the tide turned against him, and before they realized what was happening there he was, one more convicted felon in the crucifixion annals of Rome. You talk about "broken things, too broke to mend," this was the mood of his followers that Sabbath eve as they hurriedly laid his body in a borrowed tomb before the sun went down. More than one woman crumpled to the ground in tears that night. At the point where they had come to expect so much, suddenly it was all over. There seemed to be no future for this Jesus or for his followers. What Jerusalem and Rome had succeeded in breaking, seemed for all the world "too broke to mend."

Then the absolutely unexpected occurred. Early on Sunday morning a group of women made their way to the tomb to finish the job that time had not permitted on Friday afternoon. But when they got there, the stone was rolled back and the tomb was empty. It did not occur to them at first that what they were encountering was something God had done. They looked on it as yet another expression of human depravity, one more tragedy in a long string of atrocities. They assumed that graverobbers had added insult to injury by taking the body that had been crucified and further desecrating it. "Where have you laid his body? If you will only tell us we will go and get it." This was the extent of their concern, the only hope they had, when suddenly he appeared and said "Mary" as only he would say it, and then it began to dawn:

Jesus was not dead any longer! The body that had been killed on Friday had been raised back to life! The empty tomb that they were looking at was not the work of graverobbers. It was the work of God! They could hardly grasp it. Jesus was alive again and back in the world!

According to one account (Mark 16:1-8), he told the women to go and "tell the disciples and Peter" that he was alive and was going ahead of them into Galilee where the great adventure had first begun. He wanted all of them to meet him there, because it was time to get on with the mission — the great task of reconciling the world back to the Father. Suddenly where there had been only a past and a present, a new future emerged. What they thought was over and done with — a broken thing too broke to mend — was very much alive and well, and this was the event that literally turned things around for the disciples and gave them a whole new perspective on life.

For one thing, the Easter event reminded them all over again that God is a factor to be reckoned with as you think about the future. This is something we so easily forget in the hurly-burly of life. We tend to look at things "horizontally," as if our strength and wisdom are the only forces at work in history. We are like those women making their way through the dawn, worrying about the grave stone and how they were going to move it. It presented a challenge far beyond their resources. But when they got there — what did they find? It had been rolled away! Why? Because there is also God in the drama of history! He too plays a part in what is possible and impossible out there ahead of us, and what kind of God is he? The Easter-event speaks directly to this. Saint Paul sums it up by describing him as "the one who can make the things that are out of the things that are not, and the one who can make dead things come to life again" (Romans 4:17). Translated functionally, this means that there is both a power and a mercy in God beyond anything that we can imagine. Think about it. He was able to take a dead body, out of which all vitality had been crushed, and cause that one to live again. It is akin to what he did in the beginning when there was nothing, and he called all things into being by his mighty power. The fact that God could raise Jesus back to life again is an insight into his power and a sheer astonishment.

An even greater miracle, in my judgment, is that he should even want to do so, given how the world had treated his Son. The mercy and patience and determination to bless implicit in the Easter-event are beyond my comprehension. Let me ask you for a moment to use your imagination. What if you found a problem family and decided to try to help them get on their feet? You provide them a place to live, get them work, go out of your way to assist them — but they only grow worse. They refuse to work, tear up your house, and reduce everything to shambles. You call in other helpers — social workers, county agents, doctors — but they still refuse all kinds of assistance. Then your only son comes in and says: "I still think these people can be helped. Let me try. When they realize who I am and all our family has done, surely they will let me help straighten things out." So he goes, and word comes back to you that they did not just run him off like the rest — they tied him up and tortured him and finally killed him in cold blood.

I ask you: How would you feel at this point toward people who were capable of such inhumanity? Would you consider them worthless and hopeless? If you had it in your power to raise that boy from the dead, would it ever occur to you to send him back to those same people? Of course not! Blasting such ingrates back to nothingness would be more appropriate. Yet can you believe that on the first Easter, this is exactly what God did? By calling for the disciples and Peter to meet him in Galilee, God manifests mercy, patience, and a hope for our kind that is absolutely unbelievable. He did not give up on the people who crucified his Son! He still had affection and hope for them!

This is the kind of God who made himself known at Easter — the power and the mercy "who can make the things that are out of the things that are not, and who can make dead things come to life again." And if this is the one to be factored in as you contemplate the future, do you not see what this does to despair? Who are we to look down on our broken things and say: "Too broke to mend"? If God was not only able but willing to take the broken body of Jesus and raise it back to life, what can't he do — what lives, what marriages, what families, what careers can't he mend? The functional effect of Easter is to change forever the way we use the words "possible" and "impossible." If there is also God out there in the future, then despair is not only presumptuous, it is downright heretical and even sinful.

I say despair is presumptuous, not because of Easter, but because of the limits of human knowledge. Saint Paul once said that "we know in part and prophesy in part" that our seeing is "as through a glass darkly." In other words, we humans do not know enough about the depths of reality to pontificate about what can or cannot be in the future. Over and over again I have been amazed by people and events. From my perspective a situation looked absolutely hopeless, only to have factors emerge out of the depths that I had no idea were present.

Apart from any knowledge of Easter, absolute despair is presumptuous, for it is concluding something about a situation that we finite humans have no right to conclude. Before Easter, then, despair is presumptuous, but after Easter, it is downright heretical and even sinful. Why? Because it ignores this God "who can make the things that are out of the things that are not, and who can make dead things come to life again." It is approaching all those heavy grave stones out in the future as if our strength is all that is available. It is looking at all the broken things within us and about us and concluding that because we cannot do anything about them, they are "too broke to mend." But listen, you do not have to go on living this way, for Easter has happened, which means out there in the future there is also God, and not just any God, but one who had power enough to raise Jesus back from the dead and mercy enough to send him back to his crucifiers. This is why I say despair is heretical and downright sinful. And even more, it is so unnecessary!

One of the greatest sermons Carlyle Marney, the late great preacher and professor, ever preached is titled "God's Strong Hands." It is about Judas and the ultimate tragedy of his life. His undoing, Marney said, lay not in his decision to betray our Lord, dastardly as that was, but in not staying around to see what God could do with human defection. In other words, Judas' greatest sin was the sin of despair. When the full impact of what he had done finally hit him, it was more than he could stand. He seemed to himself "a broken thing, too broke to mend," a creature so contemptible as to be utterly beyond mercy. And so he took his own life — the most obvious thing to do when it appears there is no future left.

What a pity, says Marney, what a gross underestimation of what God's strong hands can do with human brokenness. If he had only waited around for the final act of that awful drama — to Easter Sunday — then undoubtedly he would have heard the women exclaim: "Jesus said to go and tell the disciples and Peter and Judas I want to meet them in Galilee and get on with it." After all, what Judas did was not that much worse than what Peter did when he denied our Lord or the others when they deserted him. There would have been mercy enough even for Judas. I am sure of that. But he did not stay around to see what God can do with what we have done. He despaired. He forgot that out there in the future there is also God powerful enough to make dead things come to life again and mercy enough to be willing to do so.

Please learn from Judas and do not make the same mistake. I know a lot of things may seem broken just now — hopes, careers, families, marriages. I know for some of you the future looks dreary — nothing but a lot of grave stones out there too heavy for you to move. But listen, there is also God! There is also Pentecost that not only gives us hope but also gives us mission, a mission that has a great factor in the shaping of tomorrow. It is with this power of the Holy Spirit that the plan all comes together and we can see the despair, the victory, and now the power to go into a world that is being given new life. There is power enough and mercy enough in the Holy Spirit through Jesus to deal with whatever brokenness you brought to this place today. When Jesus said to go tell the disciples and Peter, they would come to know it wasn't over at all, even with the resurrection. Now the power was in their hands to show the world. It is now into ours, and before us is the future. We then ask on Pentecost: "What broken thing is there too broke to mend? Nothing, nothing at all. Listen, there is a future for us all. There is hope. There is also God!" Hallelujah!

Holy Trinity Sunday
Matthew 28:16-20

As You Go, Remember...

Now the eleven disciples went to Galilee, to the mountain to which Jesus had directed them. When they saw him, they worshiped him; but some doubted. And Jesus came and said to them, "All authority in heaven and on earth has been given to me. Go therefore and make disciples of all nations, baptizing them in the name of the Father and of the Son and of the Holy Spirit, and teaching them to obey everything that I have commanded you. And remember, I am with you always, to the end of the age."

What intrigues us the most is that mysterious boundary where the human and the divine intersect. This was the place I said I wanted to plant my life and to do my central work. This was, in fact, living out the charge that was given to me the night I was ordained to the Christian ministry. I still remember the way an old pastor stated it. He said, "Tom, I admonish you to stay close to God, stay close to humankind, and to make it the goal of your ministry to bring God and humankind closer together." This really has been my "bottom-line objective" in all I have tried to do.

More than anything else, I have wanted to heighten awareness of the God-reality and facilitate a relation of trust and interaction between the two that takes the aloneness out of human existence. It is my theological assumption that each of us is related to God already. We are "sons and daughters of the most high," not because of anything we have done but because of what he has done in creating us. Therefore, the religious challenge is always to help people become aware of what already is rather than having to create a relationship from scratch. Let's face it, the prodigal did not become his father's son through what happened to him in the far country. That experience of "coming to himself" represented an awakening to what had always been the case, but up to that point had not been realized or accepted. My great goal, then, has been to open blind eyes and unstop deaf ears, to make us aware at deeper and deeper levels of who we really are and who our source in heaven truly is, to get a more vital and personal interaction moving between the two.

A friend of mine in Nashville had an experience several years ago that lets us see in a graphic way what I have wanted to accomplish. He entered a large department store one day and heard considerable commotion around one of the counters and saw a four-year-old child obviously lost from her parents crying hysterically. The store officials were trying frantically to get some information from the little girl. Fortunately, my friend recognized her. She was the daughter of one of his classmates in college. Therefore, he went straight to the public address system in the store and said very clearly, "Will Jane and Jack Jones, the parents of Mary Anne, please come to counter 26 immediately. Your child is safe and waiting here."

In a matter of minutes, my friend witnessed the coming together of distraught parents and a frightened child. As they grasped each other joyfully, my friend reported genuine satisfaction at having played a part in this event of reuniting. This little episode mirrors exactly what I have wanted to facilitate. You see, I happen "to recognize" each one of you. I know who you are. Jesus is the name of your species, and none other than God almighty himself is your source and parent. I also have some sense of how much richer life could be if it were done "two by two" and every moment of it a sharing with that kind of wisdom and love and strength.

This has been my foremost agenda: "To stay close to God, to stay close to each person, and to do what I could to bring the two closer together." And this explains, I suppose, why I have ended most services on Sunday morning with the words: "Depart now, in the fellowship of God the Father...." What I have wanted to do is to contribute, like my friend, in getting God and his children back together again. That is the primal event, and I trust you realize that everything else in that benediction is simply a description of what that kind of "coming together again" involves.

For example, once you begin to be aware of the God-reality, it becomes clear that your being born into this world was something infinitely good. In the book of Genesis you find a faith story, which claims that all creation comes out of God's positive desire to share the godness. God found God's own aliveness so overwhelmingly positive that God said: "This is too good to keep to myself. I want others to experience it too." Thus this creation story was not a cruel joke. It was not done irresponsibly. It was an act of positive intentionality, and Genesis goes on today in that God is utterly pleased with what God has created. Again and again you find the refrain: "And God looked on what God had made and behold it was very, very good." I believe that Christian redemption begins when we come to feel about the event of our own creation the same way Genesis depicts God feeling about all that God has made: "It is good. It is good. It is very, very good." The deeper you move into God-consciousness, the more that evaluation of creation will become true.

This primal goodness is not just present at the beginning. "By the grace of God, you have been kept, all the day long, even until this hour." There is a mercy in the unfolding of history that is just as great as the goodness that lies behind it. When we stop to think of all of the things that could have happened to us up to this moment, all the diseases we could have contracted, the accidents in which we could have been involved, then we realize how slender is the thread that sustains us all! The fact that we are still breathing, still alive in the here and now, is as towering a miracle as being born out of nothing, and it all goes back to the grace of God. As the familiar hymn: "Amazing Grace" puts it: "Through many hardships, toils, and snares we have already come, 'tis grace has brought us safe thus far, and grace will lead us home."

What is it all for? "In the love of God, fully revealed, in the face of Jesus, you are being redeemed." This part of the prayer pertains to the future, and to what ultimately God intends to do if we will let him. The word "redeem" literally means "to buy back" so that one can fully complete and develop. Hosea "redeemed" his wife Gomer from slavery. Yahweh "redeemed" his people Israel from out of Egypt. All the mercy, patience, and persistence of one who having begun a good work wants to see it through to completion is bound up in the ancient term. And it suggests to me the vision that God sets before all of us as his intended objective. In Jesus Christ, he has made manifest in history what a fully functioning human being would be like, and the goal now in the slow process of life is to continue to work with us until we too attain to "the measure of the stature of the fullness of Christ." In the face of Jesus we see our species brought to its highest expression, and we know that if God has his final way, he will some day make each of us into that kind of perfection.

I refer to the last verse in our text, which is usually translated as an imperative. In the original Greek, the future and the imperative are spelled exactly alike, so that on textual grounds it could just as well be translated as a promise rather than a command; namely, "I will let you in on my ultimate objective." It is not something we have to attain before God begins to do anything with us. It is what God intends to create at the end of our lives if we will allow him. The only thing that can impede that process is our failure of heart and our unwillingness to allow the full sweep of grace to do its work. I often think the crucial issue in life is this: "How much or how little will we settle for?" The great enemy here is not God's wrath or impatience, but our timidity and fearfulness, our unwillingness to expose ourselves to that tough and tender mercy that has it in its power to bring us to fullness.

C.S. Lewis used to say that whenever he got a toothache as a child, he was always faced with the painful dilemma of whether or not to tell his mother. On the one hand, if he told her, he knew she would give him an aspirin and thus what he most wanted; namely, temporary relief from his pain. However, the problem was that she would not stop there. She would get to the bottom of the toothache, which meant going to the dentist, the drill, and all of that, and all he really wanted was relief in the moment. He really did not want to undergo a thorough resolution.

This spirit is the greatest enemy of God's good goal; we humans are willing to settle for so little, so tempted "to keep one foot on the bottom," to cling to the tiny securities and achievements that we have in hand, rather than casting ourselves into the great sweep of his mercies, assured that no matter how much pain and uncertainty we may endure, the goal of making us full-grown and complete is assured. This is a process that has already begun and is in motion now, but is not yet complete. Yet I must warn that we have a crucial role to play in whether or not the grand design of God finally comes true in our own lives. God wants to make us full-grown and complete, but God cannot without our consent and collaboration.

The journey is never over. We move ever so slowly at times but are always reminded in the most powerful way of the great love that was good enough to enable us to be born into this world, gracious enough to spare us all the day long, even until this hour, and persistent and merciful enough to redeem us finally, keep us from falling, and present us complete and full-grown at last before God. As we consider this passage may it awaken us to this reality that surrounds our lives. God is, you are, and the two of you are made for each other. It is enough that we should die alone. There is no need to live alone. The journey can be shared with God. Therefore, go, go with God, be not afraid.

Proper 7
Pentecost 2
Ordinary Time 12
Matthew 10:24-39

Death, Risk, and Confidence

A disciple is not above the teacher, nor a slave above the master; it is enough for the disciple to be like the teacher, and the slave like the master. If they have called the master of the house Beelzebul, how much more will they malign those of his household! So have no fear of them; for nothing is covered up that will not be uncovered, and nothing secret that will not become known. What I say to you in the dark, tell in the light; and what you hear whispered, proclaim from the housetops. Do not fear those who kill the body but cannot kill the soul; rather fear him who can destroy both soul and body in hell. Are not two sparrows sold for a penny? Yet not one of them will fall to the ground apart from your Father. And even the hairs of your head are all counted. So do not be afraid; you are of more value than many sparrows. Everyone therefore who acknowledges me before others, I also will acknowledge before my Father in heaven; but whoever denies me before others, I also will deny before my Father in heaven. Do not think that I have come to bring peace to the earth; I have not come to bring peace, but a sword. For I have come to set a man against his father, and a daughter against her mother, and a daughter-in-law against her mother-in-law; and one's foes will be members of one's own household. Whoever loves father or mother more than me is not worthy of me; and whoever loves son or daughter more than me is not worthy of me; and whoever does not take up the cross and follow me is not worthy of me. Those who find their life will lose it, and those who lose their life for my sake will find it.

I shall never forget a most vivid pastoral encounter that I had. There was a fine older member of the church who was terminally ill with cancer, and since he would never be able to come and meet me, I went by his home to meet him. Although we had never met before, I suppose my role prompted him to get right to the central issue of his concern at that moment, which was with the whole experience of death. He wanted to know what I believed lay beyond the experience of dying. He was concerned about guilt and several other matters of unfinished business, and although I was young at the time and had not yet myself been initiated into "the fraternity of the grievers," I did my very best to respond to him honestly and felt it was one of the most significant and poignant human encounters that I have ever known.

His wife was in and out of the room several times as we talked, and as I made my way to leave she walked with me out in the garden and said very emotionally: "Young man, don't you ever do again what you did this afternoon. We are doing our best to cheer Daddy up and to keep his spirits high. Things are bad enough as they are without all this morbid talk about dying. I don't want that word ever used again in his presence. Unless you can make me that promise, I will not let you come back again."

I was really not surprised at either one of these reactions. Dr. Elizabeth Kübler-Ross, a person who has researched death and the events around death, claims that the dying almost always know that they are dying and this awareness often prompts them to lay aside "the conspiracy of silence" that our culture has constructed about death and reach out to others and attempt to share their feelings and finish the business at hand before it is too late. However, those who are not in such desperate straits often have so much fear and insecurity of their own that they cannot handle such honesty, so they busily try to divert attention and cheer up the dying, so to speak, which means in effect they add the burden of loneliness to everything else the dying person is having to experience. They force them needlessly "to walk that lonesome valley all by themselves."

I think the cross-currents in which I found myself that afternoon are very typical of our American culture when it comes to the subject of death and dying, and real progress could be made for all of us if well before the actual experience of dying we could lay aside our fears and honestly "ask, seek, and knock" about what Gail Sheehy, the author of *Passages in Caregiving: Turning Chaos into Confidence*, calls "the dark at the end of the tunnel," that moment of the great relinquishment we call physical death. Maybe if more education had been given to this couple that I mentioned earlier, the dying man would not have been so panicky, nor would the wife have been so frightened that she could not offer companionship. Therefore, I make no apologies for what I am doing in raising directly the issue of death and dying and suggesting we look at it honestly and openly. After all, it seems in our culture of instant media we are confronted with death every day in one way or another. But more importantly, we will be better equipped, not only for dying but also for living and sharing with others, if we will face now the questions and fears and uncertainties that rise up in us at the prospect of our ceasing to be alive in history. The more we put this off the less able we will be to handle the challenge creatively. The more work we are willing to do now, the better it will be for us in the future.

Maybe we can approach this with steady eyes and look straight at the basic issue involved in this phenomenon. What happens to a person when that one experiences physical death and passes from this realm of earthly existence? Obviously, we can describe the physical and material dimensions of the experience. The body remains here as well as all of one's material possessions. "There are no pockets in a shroud," as the Arab proverb puts it. We do not take anything physical or material with us on this journey. It represents a stripping away of these aspects of personality, a "going through the eye of the needle," as Douglas Steere, who was a long-time professor of philosophy at Haverford College, describes it. Only the animating spirit of a person leaves — that willing, thinking, reflecting inner self. This seems to be the only vessel left in which to embark on whatever sea lies beyond this experience. We have no more physical or material power with which to work at such a moment. If there is anything more, it is up to another, and the question arises: "Does another power exist at all, and if so, is it the sort of power that cherishes individuals and would want or would be able to sustain such spirits and enable them to live on in other realms?" The moment of death is just like the moment of birth in terms of who is there to receive and nurture and develop these "bare selves" who cannot sustain themselves. This really is the issue: "After death, what? Is there or is there not a receiving, sustaining, nurturing presence who will give us life-after-death on the same terms we were given life-after-birth?"

I trust you realize that the New Testament eloquently declares that such a power does exist and can be counted on in the moment of the great relinquishment. The love that called us out of nothing into being is at once larger than life and stronger than death. We are told that it is not the will of the Father that any should perish, but that all should come to the fullness of his purpose. The book claims that nothing, not even the experience of death, can separate us from the love that is in Christ Jesus our Lord. In fact, the New Testament depicts Christ as that courageous figure who did not just walk into the valley of the shadow of death but through that valley to the light on the other side, and having done that he came back to say to us: "Be not afraid of death. There is only God and he can be trusted." What is more, Christ has now positioned himself like a ferryman at the great divide, and promises "having gone to prepare a place for us, that he will come again and receive us unto himself"; that is, he will traverse that "space between the worlds" with us and beside us. "Lo, I am with you always, even to the ends of the earth" were his words, which means that when you have nothing and can do nothing — exactly as you were when you were born — there will be one to receive you and sustain you and nurture you as there was when you came out of your mother's womb. And realize — it is all of grace. We do not earn the gift of life after death anymore than we earned our way into this world at birth. It is all of grace, not of works, lest any person should boast. Here, then, is the New Testament witness to the question "After death, what then?" It points to a love that is larger than life and stronger than death, the same love that created us in the beginning, and this leads us to question "What is the basis for accepting or rejecting such a claim?" Here is what the New Testament says about the mystery of death. What am I to say as response to this?

I believe there are two alternatives at this point. A person can simply accept this vision of reality on the authority of Holy Scripture. The written word does have the power to come alive for us to convince us of its reality. After all, we would never know the incredible story of God's love and suffering on our behalf if it were not for the book. Therefore, simply on the basis that we have found it trustworthy in the past, one can accept what it teaches about the future with perfect confidence. John Baillie, the Scottish theologian, tells of a doctor who was called one day to the home of a dying friend. As he sat quietly by this one, suddenly the dying man sat up in horror and cried, "Tell me, friend, what is it going to be like to die? What is the next world like? Is there friend or foe to be encountered there?" The doctor recognized that the man was in mortal terror, and he prayed for some means to convey to him a sense of hope. At that very moment there was a scratching at the door, and the doctor's prayer was answered. He said softly to his friend, "Did you hear that noise just then? That was my old dog Shep who walked over here with me from home. He has no idea what lies in this room or the other side of the door. He has never been here and has no information about what it is like. All he knows is that I am here. He can hear my voice, and he has learned to trust in me. I really do not know exactly what it is like to die or what 'the world beyond the world' is like. But I do know that Jesus has given us his word that he will be there, and because that is true there is nothing to fear. How could you describe to a fetus in the mother's womb what time and space are like? They are not ready for that yet. So Jesus did not give us information about the next life, just the promise to meet us at the border and take us to the place he has already prepared." It proved to be a word of hope. On the authority of Holy Scripture, this man was given to believe that what he was about to experience was not walking out on a pier and dropping into nothingness, but rather venturing onto a bridge, where there already was another and in whose company the transition would be made from realm to realm. You can then let the authority of the book be the basis of your hope.

However, there is another way, not altogether separate from the first, but different nonetheless — the way of risking obedience long before the trauma of dying, and learning in your own experience that there is another who can be depended on and who is able to sustain. Jesus said again and again, "Whosoever would save his life will lose it, but whosoever would lose his life for my sake and the gospel's, will save it." I think he is talking about those occasions in life where we dare to risk beyond the security that our own strength and our own material possessions can provide, to step out in faith, not knowing the end from the beginning, not having everything in our knapsack that we feel we are going to need, but like Abraham, moved from beyond, we venture to the limit of our own powers, only to discover that we are not alone, that there is another, and we are received in those moments as surely as we were received when we came from our mothers' wombs. What I am suggesting is that all "the little deaths" we undergo as we dare to risk and venture may teach more about the sufficiency of God in the act of dying than a thousand abstract ideas.

    I have known several people in my life who were no longer afraid of either death or life. They were really courageous and alive and spontaneous folk, and in every case they had come to this robust confidence through the experience of risk and venture. They had, on occasion, begun something when they did not know the end from the beginning, did not have all the resources in hand before setting out, and it was this very daring to go to the limits that enabled them to discover that one who is in fact there and can do something when we get to the place we cannot. This is a discovery you can never make if you forever hug the shore and keep one foot on the bottom, obsessed with creating your own security. This is the way of trying to save life that ends up losing it. You never discover for yourself that the waters of God's grace will hold you up because you have never lifted your foot from the bottom and dared to float. If this has been your style of life from day one, no wonder death seems such a terror, for remember, it is a stripping away of the material and physical aspects of personality — it is "going through the eye of a needle" where there is nothing left but you and God, and if you never have been without your security before, what a terror!

    I remember once going to the intensive care unit where a lady in my congregation was hovering near death after a devastating heart attack. I have never in all my life seen such terror on a face amid all those tubes and monitoring instruments, and I had real trouble mediating any real comfort to this person, for you see, all her life she had been pampered and protected and shielded from risk. She had come from a wealthy family and had a husband who treated her more like a doll or a toy than a sturdy human being, and as a result she was totally unprepared for the great venture in trust that is the essence of dying.

The more we avoid risk and venture in the days of our living, the less prepared we are to face death with confidence. It is in the attempts to save our lives that we lose the opportunity to learn of this power, and it is in the experience of losing our lives for Christ's sake and the gospel's that we discover the amazing grace that can do things for us when we cannot do anymore for ourselves.

This thought brings me back to where it all started — our ambivalent feelings about life's greatest inevitability — the experience of death. Run from it as we try, we cannot help but wonder: "What is it going to be like? Is there nothing or something when we become totally helpless again? Is death a pier or a bridge?"

Jesus always points to hope. God, who made all things, loves all that God has made. It is not God's will that any should perish. But how are we to believe that? You can take the Bible's word for it, and that is significant indeed. In addition, you can test in your own experience a venture of obedience — launching out where you do not know the end from the beginning, and in such risk, finding it is true: There is no fleeing from God's loving presence. "If I ascend up into heaven, lo, he is there. If I make my bed in Sheol, he is there. Lo, if I take the wings of the morning and flee to the uttermost parts of the sea, even there his right hand holds me, his right hand sustains me." It is "perfect love that casteth out fear," and you do not have to wait until you die to begin to experience it. On the other side of risk is discovery and help. If you try to save your own life, you will lose it. But those who dare to lose their lives for Christ's sake — ah — they are the ones that find that he can save.

You do not have to wait. Learn the secret of dying now. It is also the secret of living.

Proper 8
Pentecost 3
Ordinary Time 13
Matthew 10:40-42

Jesus Morality

> Whoever welcomes you welcomes me, and whoever welcomes me welcomes the one who sent me. Whoever welcomes a prophet in the name of a prophet will receive a prophet's reward; and whoever welcomes a righteous person in the name of a righteous person will receive the reward of the righteous; and whoever gives even a cup of cold water to one of these little ones in the name of a disciple — truly I tell you, none of these will lose their reward.

There is one question that every one of us has to deal with at least a hundred times a day and that is "What ought I to do in this given moment?" Sometimes the issues at stake are far-reaching, such as with the questions "Should I ask her to marry me?" or "Should I go into law or medicine or the ministry?" At other times the issues are less momentous, such as "Do I want toast or cereal for breakfast?" or "Do I wear khakis or jeans today?" However, in each case a process of evaluating and choosing between alternatives takes place, and nothing is of any more concrete significance to our lives than how we go about making our decisions. Historically, this aspect of life has been denoted by the word "morality," and it is not surprising that debates have raged in every era on how this process of decision-making should be conducted. Our age is no exception, for in the last several years much has been said and written about the so-called "new morality" or situational ethics, and I would like for us to look at this debate in the hope that we can sharpen our own insight into how best to handle the challenges of our lives as we make concrete decisions every day.

As I view the current discussion in the field of Christian ethics, there seem to be two distinct approaches to the question. For example, there are an impressive number of moralists who say that the most important thing to be considered in decision-making is the principle or rule or law that had been established in the past. These people are concerned with the wisdom that has been distilled down through the ages. By both revelation and experience, certain guidelines to behavior have emerged, and this group feels that the answers to any present dilemma can be found by looking to the past and finding a precedent that prescribes what one ought to do under given circumstances. The emphasis here is largely on the continuity of life — the past being looked on as holding the key to the present and the future. The crucial factor in this way of deciding is thus external or outside the immediate situation. When I find myself having to act in a particular set of circumstances, the thing for me to do is to look back and find the rule out of the past that corresponds to this situation and then apply it. Some have characterized this as "a yellow pages" approach to morality. When a decision has to be made, consult the wisdom of the past and find there the appropriate prescription.

On the other side of the modern debate is a group of moralists who start from a very different point of reference. They make the persons involved rather than principles their primary concern, and tend to look to the future rather than the past as the more important time-zone. For example, when faced with several alternatives, instead of saying "What are the precedents here, the rules out of the past to be followed?" these people would ask: "What about the persons in this situation? How can the greatest good to the largest number of people be brought about here?" Instead of looking at the present in terms of the past, this approach tends to look at the present in light of the future, and asks the question: "Since my action is going to make a difference in the situation before me, what can I do here and now that will bring the greatest good to the most people?" Because of its emphasis on the present and the immediate, this approach is sometimes called "situational ethics," but this term can be misleading, for the ultimate point of reference is not just the variables of the situation but a genuine concern for persons and how their interests can best be served in light of the actualities of the now. In this approach to morality, there is a deep suspicion of any kind of prescriptive law or principle. These people feel that each day is a new creation and not exactly like anything before. Thus, new situations call for new solutions. The wineskins of olden times may not be adequate for what is new and unique in the present.

I certainly would not claim that this is a complete summary of the debate on "the new morality," but I believe the shape of the controversy can be detected. On the one hand, there are those who make principles or rules their determining points of reference, and thus move into the sphere of decision-making with one eye on the present and the other on the past. Over against this approach are those who make human persons the focus of their concern, and thus move into the arena with one eye on the present and the other on the future.

Now what are folks like you and me to make of all of this, and how does it relate to the very practical matter of how we make our moral decisions day by day? I tend to agree with Professor James Gustafson that the controversy here is really misplaced, for I find a significant truth in both of these approaches; yet neither one of them is adequate by itself or apart from the other. There are actually several factors involved in authentic moral decision-making, and to absolutize one aspect to the exclusion of the other always upsets the balance of truth and leads to distortion.

In my judgment, this is what both of the extreme positions I have described have done. To focus on principles and the past alone without an equal concern for persons and the future can produce real problems. By the same token, however, a concern for person and the future that is divorced from the wisdom of the past can be very superficial. If one's moral perspective is to be balanced at all, both of these concerns need to be held together in creative tension — and we get a glimpse of this very thing happening as we observe the teaching of Jesus in our text with an instruction that seems as clear as any in the Bible as to the decision to welcome others and give hospitality. In Matthew's gospel, all of the issues in the current ethical debate are present and highly visible, and we can learn a great deal as Jesus' teaching uses the simplest gestures in these moments of decision-making.

Jesus outlines the whole idea of welcoming in a most logical way. It seems like something we all should do or be doing. However, we should revisit the concept of "welcome" to get a fresh idea of what that looked like in the day of Jesus, and how it looks today. The problem seems to come when we realize how ambiguous the word "welcome" happens to be. It is a matter of acceptance and non-acceptance. Matthew probably assumes that the person who extends hospitality to a prophet is himself or herself a believer. The one receiving a prophet is generously promised a reward equal to that awaiting the prophet. It does not seem like a stretch to welcome a prophet or a righteous person. I think the rub comes when we get to the last couple of lines of this: "Whoever gives even a cup of cold water to one of these little ones in the name of a disciple." First, who are the little ones? Second, what does it mean to give a cup of cold water to a person like this? It is obvious in Matthew that the "little ones" are children or people who cannot fully take care of themselves. Here in a few words we have the mission of the gospel spoken by Jesus.

I was wondering how that would look today if we were to move this teaching of Jesus to the 21st century, when we find ourselves embroiled in an ethical decision. A number of years ago the church I was pastoring supported a "Free Medical Clinic" that was a service to the community where it was located and did amazing work among those who had very little income. Our contribution had grown through the years to the amount of a major donor. It was always a discussion at budget time, however there was always someone present who was totally invested in the mission of our church. One particular year we had a meeting of the budget committee and the trustees, and to my surprise the meeting was almost over and no one had mentioned cutting the support to the clinic. I was waiting for an "Amen" and I could go home happy. Just as we were getting ready to leave one of the "bean counters" pushed his chair back and said, "We need to talk about all this money we are giving away to this clinic. I am not so sure we should be sending them anything."

My heart sank as I thought of the fight before us. Just then one person to whom everyone always listened spoke up: "Instead of deciding this without any current information why don't some of us make a visit to the clinic and take the director to lunch?" Everyone agreed, and those going on the visit were the wise woman, the man with the objection, and me.

The day came for the appointment, and we arrived together about fifteen minutes early as the waiting room was clearing out. The director was also the doctor at the clinic. We sat down to wait and the receptionist told us the doctor would be out soon, but just then a woman with two children in tow came in. One child looked to be about three, and the other was a baby. She told the little three-year-old girl to sit in the waiting room until Mommy could talk to the doctor with her little brother. When the mother closed the door, the little girl looked at all of us and without a word went to the man who was against supporting the clinic. She climbed up into his lap and snuggled in for a nap. He held the little girl until the mother returned and as the mother took the little girl she held onto the man. Finally when the girl let his hand go, she said "Bye…you are comfortable…bye-bye."

When we arrived at the café for lunch and we listened as the doctor told us all that was going on with the clinic, to my surprise the man who had been against supporting it said, "Well, you can count on us for our continued support and we will add to what we have been doing."

As that event closed it brought to my mind what Jesus said "…whoever gives even a cup of cold water to one of these little ones in the name of a disciple." I think that day we saw the teaching of Jesus come alive.

I think this is really Jesus Morality!

Proper 9
Pentecost 4
Ordinary Time 14
Matthew 11:16-19, 25-30

What Do You Bring to the Table?

But to what will I compare this generation? It is like children sitting in the marketplaces and calling to one another, "We played the flute for you, and you did not dance; we wailed, and you did not mourn." For John came neither eating nor drinking, and they say, "He has a demon"; the Son of Man came eating and drinking, and they say, "Look, a glutton and a drunkard, a friend of tax collectors and sinners!" Yet wisdom is vindicated by her deeds.... At that time Jesus said, "I thank you, Father, Lord of heaven and earth, because you have hidden these things from the wise and the intelligent and have revealed them to infants"; yes, Father, for such was your gracious will. All things have been handed over to me by my Father; and no one knows the Son except the Father, and no one knows the Father except the Son and anyone to whom the Son chooses to reveal him. "Come to me, all you that are weary and are carrying heavy burdens, and I will give you rest. Take my yoke upon you, and learn from me; for I am gentle and humble in heart, and you will find rest for your souls. For my yoke is easy, and my burden is light."

When we fly we are well aware of the fact that you cannot simply go out and buy a ticket and get on an airplane anymore. Nowadays, because of all the skyjacking and dangers, there is an elaborate system of surveillance before you get near an aircraft. Understandably, the authorities want to know what you are bringing with you to the plane. And so your own person and everything you are carrying is carefully examined.

As I found myself thinking about our communion, I wondered what it would be like if there were some spiritual counterpart to the security checks at the airport. If we had some way of discerning what kind of spiritual burdens a person carries into the sanctuary, what do you suppose would be discovered?

I am sure that when some people step across the threshold into the sanctuary, there is brought a burden of grief in one form or another. Carlyle Marney, an author, pastor, and professor, once began a communion meditation by looking out over the congregation and saying, "What a bunch of losers we all are." He was not using that term "loser" in its competitive sense. He was using it to acknowledge the many kinds of grief we have all experienced. There probably is not anyone over ten years old who has not known the agony of being separated prematurely from something that is valued highly, be that a mate or a parent or a dog or ring or job or something. Miguel Unamuno, a Spanish essayist, novelist, poet, playwright, and philosopher, says in his most famous novel *Abel Sánchez: The History of a Passion*, "All grief comes back to this one thing. We run out of time." This is true of all of us. The golden moments "when you would have liked to have lived forever" come to an end all too soon. Therefore, one by one we all become "persons of sorrow, acquainted with grief." It is true — in our own way we are "a bunch of losers," each and every one of us. And I wonder, is grief the overwhelming burden that people bring with them into a sanctuary?

Then again, I am confident that a spiritual detector would have picked up all kinds of guilt coming into a sanctuary. Paul writes in Romans that we have all sinned, not just some of us, but all of us have fallen short of the glory of God. Though we do not like to talk about it or to focus our attention on it, by day and by night we live in an atmosphere that is seasoned with guilt. Paul Tournier, Swiss physician, author, and pastoral counselor, tells about a pathetic man who was so burdened by his past that he used to walk down the streets of Geneva and say to every person he met, "I'm sorry. I'm sorry." These words summed up his whole life. Many people, at least in part, identify with that sense of great regret. Most of us, if not all, have felt pangs of guilt as far as our children or parents or work or wife or husband or country or church are concerned. Unless I am badly mistaken, guilt of all shapes and forms goes through sanctuary doors every minute of every day. It seems that we have "done those things that we should not have done, and we have left undone the things we should have done." In relation to sinless perfection, "there is no health in us." Maybe guilt is the burden most of us bring with us into a place of worship. Then again, I am sure there is a good bit of seething rage also. It is evident on all sides and in relation to many situations. Some people are angry at the whole shape of the universe and at the God who is responsible for it all.

After seeing member after member of his family disintegrate in tragedy, Eugene O'Neill, the Irish-American playwright and Nobel laureate in literature, said: "I can partly understand how God can forgive human beings, for we are so weak and vulnerable. But what I cannot understand is how he can ever forgive himself for creating a world like this." That is an anger of an ultimate sort, directed at no less than God. And there are many forms of rage this side of such ultimacy. There are many today who are angry because they are women in a world that is still largely dominated and controlled by men. By the same token, others are resentful of the toll being a male has taken on them, having to work hard and die young while their wives eat lunch at the women's club and do as they please. There are other people who are angry at having to grow old in a society that worships the young, at being made constantly to feel that their ideas are out of date and their continued presence a burden. There are all kinds of anger in the atmosphere today, and in all honesty, this is part of what is brought with people that enter sanctuaries all over the world.

Then again, perhaps what we feel is not as positive as any of this; that is just the problem, we feel nothing at all except boredom, emptiness, and inward deadness. Not long ago a third-generation millionaire in North Carolina took his life at the age of 57 and left behind a simple note that read in part: "I've been everywhere. I've done everything. I've tasted it all, looked at it all, possessed and grown weary of it all. There is nothing left. I quit." This is a heightened form of the feeling I sense in a lot of people today. I have had adult after adult look at me and ask, "Is this all? Do I have nothing more to look forward to than this marriage partner, this house, this job, this universe?" Somewhere between forty and fifty the light of expectation goes out for a host of people, and then we wonder how many this applies to. We ask ourselves if the thing we bring to the sanctuary is a sense of inner deadness, boredom, and emptiness?

Repeating again: If there were some sort of spiritual surveillance instrument comparable to what you step through at the airport, it is with confidence that we all have set off the alarm as we passed through — with grief, guilt, anger, emptiness, boredom. This in fact is where many of us are and what we bring into our place of worship. But there is good news. In a moment's time we get to move down to the table and are invited to join what we might call the great identification that has been made with us and the great invitation that is offered to us. After all, that is what holy communion is all about. It reminds us of how long ago God did not begrudge us even his Son, but sent him to enter history and become one with us — not because we deserved it, but because we needed it. He took upon himself our grief, guilt, anger, emptiness, and boredom. Yes, he drank to the last dregs all that it means to be a human being, and in the midst of that great identification he said to all of us: "Come unto me all you who labor and are heavy laden, and I will give you rest. Take my yoke upon you and learn from me, for I am gentle and lowly in heart, and you will find rest for your souls. For my yoke is easy and my burden is light." In the face of all a person brings to a sanctuary, this is an incredible offer. The Son of God says, "If you will share with me, I will share with you. If you will openly acknowledge the things that you have brought with you, and turn them over to me, I will help you bear them. Nothing is unacceptable, too dirty for me to handle. No grief or guilt or anger or boredom disqualifies one. If a person will own it and then disown it — share it with me, then I will yoke myself to you, I will get under the load alongside you and make available to you my strength and wisdom. I do not promise to remove all your burdens instantly so that life is a rose garden, but I will share your burdens with you and help you with it all. From now on, we'll do life 'two by two.' I will assist you. I will encourage you. I will teach you how to cope, and how to change what can be changed and how to endure what cannot be changed. I will offer you hope for your grief, forgiveness for your guilt, constructive outlets for your anger, and a sense of meaning for your boredom. If you will honestly bring me your 'stuff,' here is my promise — I will give you rest — refresh you by joining with you in your struggle."

George Buttrick, notable preacher and professor at Harvard University, tells a story that obviously did not make its way into the Bible, but is extremely interesting. It seems that one day Jesus came across a bird sitting on the ground in obvious frustration. The bird said that all had been well when it was young and had no heavy wings at its sides. But then these "burdens" had grown, and the bird was resentful of having them as a part of his body. Jesus neither condemned nor laughed at the bird, but responded by telling him that what felt like heavy burdens were in fact instruments of a new kind of power. Then he proceeded to show the bird how to use those wings to fly. And lo and behold what had seemed like a burden under his tutelage became a means of mounting to the sky. This is a parable, it seems, of what happens when we answer Jesus' invitation and bring our burdens to him, yoke ourselves to him, and resolve "to learn of him." He can take things that feel to us like heavy obstacles and show us how to use them as the means of moving forward. This is the kind of rest and "refreshment" that is promised here. Jesus does not say that all our burdens will be taken away, but that he will show us how to use them so that we too can "mount up with wings like eagles, run and not be weary, walk and not faint." What I am saying is that if you will honestly acknowledge this morning what you have brought into this place and willingly share it with Christ, he will accept whatever it is, no matter how distasteful, and together the two of you can do something about it.

Honestly, then, what is brought to table? Grief? Guilt? Anger? Emptiness? Something else? Nothing is unacceptable. This is his invitation: "You, there, come unto me, you who are weary and heavy laden and I will give you rest. Here, take my yoke upon you. Share it all with me, learn of me, and things can be different!" Well, what are we waiting for?

Proper 10
Pentecost 5
Ordinary Time 15
Matthew 13:1-9, 18-23

Playing One Hand

That same day Jesus went out of the house and sat beside the sea. Such great crowds gathered around him that he got into a boat and sat there, while the whole crowd stood on the beach. And he told them many things in parables, saying: "Listen! A sower went out to sow. And as he sowed, some seeds fell on the path, and the birds came and ate them up. Other seeds fell on rocky ground, where they did not have much soil, and they sprang up quickly, since they had no depth of soil. But when the sun rose, they were scorched; and since they had no root, they withered away. Other seeds fell among thorns, and the thorns grew up and choked them. Other seeds fell on good soil and brought forth grain, some a hundredfold, some sixty, some thirty. Let anyone with ears listen!... Hear then the parable of the sower. When anyone hears the word of the kingdom and does not understand it, the evil one comes and snatches away what is sown in the heart; this is what was sown on the path. As for what was sown on rocky ground, this is the one who hears the word and immediately receives it with joy; yet such a person has no root, but endures only for a while, and when trouble or persecution arises on account of the word, that person immediately falls away. As for what was sown among thorns, this is the one who hears the word, but the cares of the world and the lure of wealth choke the word, and it yields nothing. But as for what was sown on good soil, this is the one who hears the word and understands it, who indeed bears fruit and yields, in one case a hundredfold, in another sixty, and in another thirty."

In the beginning of any really significant human endeavor, be it a marriage or parenthood or a business venture, there is usually a high level of idealism and hope. We expect to do the thing we are beginning with great success. This was certainly true of Jesus' ministry. Who can read how he emerged out of Galilee saying, "The time is fulfilled, the kingdom of heaven is at hand, repent and believe the good news," and not sense the excitement and anticipation that was present in that act of beginning? And such hopefulness was not a matter of fantasy either. Incredible things did begin to happen immediately. "The common people heard Jesus gladly"; they sensed in him an authority and a vitality that was not present in other rabbis. He began to heal all kinds of diseases and quickly generated an enthusiasm that spread like wildfire throughout Galilee. This is how it all began, but then many months later — well into his ministry — we find Jesus telling the parable that is in our text, and there is a notable shift of mood to be detected here. As he spoke of the sower who went out to sow and all the factors that began to interact with that process, a new kind of realism seems to be emerging in Jesus. By this time he appears to be coming to terms with failure, with the recognition that there are many factors other than his own intentions in the great interactions of history. To use an analogy that is not very biblical but I think will be understood here, Jesus is facing up to the fact that he was playing only one hand in the great game of human existence. There were other forces besides himself around the table of life, and when it came to the formation of the final outcome, they would play a crucial role as well as his effort. In addition to the sower and the seed and the desire for a full harvest, there was also the beaten path, the rocky soil, and all that undergrowth of thorns, and these too would play a part in the eventual outcome of all this action. It is noticeable that the uttering of this parable is at the midpoint of his career, and Jesus has a clear recognition that human existence really is a complicated affair. To get anything done in our kind of world is by no means simple or easy.

Now, this is always a critical moment in any human process, when the idealism of childhood and adolescence collides head-on with the complexities of the real world. It is easy at such a moment to go from one extreme to the other. The reformer, Martin Luther, often gave his famous image that humanity is like a drunken peasant who falls off his horse on one side, only to remount and fall off on the other side. It is also our tendency to careen from one extreme to the other, which in this case would be to move from total idealism to total despair; that is, to be so bewildered by complexity and failure that one would decide to abandon the project altogether. "What's the use of doing anything," one might conclude, "in the face of so much complication?" Because of this very tendency in human nature, this particular parable is highly significant I think, because going from one extreme to the other is emphatically not what Jesus is doing here. This parable is in the end a counsel of encouragement, not of despair, encouragement that is rooted in realism rather than fantasy. Jesus moves to solid middle ground here, away from both extremes, and this becomes a place from which he can function both realistically and at the same time hopefully and creatively.

By this time in his ministry, Jesus had come home to the fact that about three out of four of the things he would like to see happen would not materialize because of factors beyond his control. Here is the humble recognition that the reach of human aspiration does exceed our ability to grasp or achieve. Three out of four of the seeds that left the sower's hand in hope did not come to flower. It is interesting to note Jesus' numbers at this point. They parallel rather accurately what is true in the realm of baseball. If you know anything about that game you realize that a batter who hits .250 is considered about an average performer. To get as high as .300 is considered exceptional, and if anybody like Ted Williams or George Brett manages to approach the .400 mark, that is regarded as legendary. But have you ever considered how much failure is involved even in such a legendary achievement? Ted Williams still made more outs than hits even during that record-setting season, which underlines how far from total perfection even the most extraordinary human efforts fall. We do ourselves a great disservice by applying perfectionistic criterion to any form of human activity. Our species was simply not built to function at such a level, and we either come to terms with this or else.

I remember vividly when a church leader approached me several years ago after worship as I was lamenting that the sermon had not really come off as I had hoped it would. He responded by saying: "You are at your best in the pulpit about ten percent of the time, about ten percent of the time you are at your worst, and the other eighty percent falls somewhere in between. Your problem is that you want every sermon to be in that top ten percent register, and that simply is an inhuman ideal. If you don't learn how to accept this fact, it's going to kill you." Those words made a deep impression, for they speak to a distortion in our mechanism of expectation that will destroy us if it is not corrected. The church leader was right. None of us is at his or her best all the time. Our capacity to rise to the heights is matched by our capacity to fall flat on our faces, and most of what we do falls somewhere in between. In this parable, I see Jesus coming to terms realistically with this characteristic of our human species, and that is a significant step of growth for any human being to take in moving out of adolescent idealism toward maturity.

But alongside this chastened sense of realism is a note of hopefulness as well. One has missed the whole point of the parable if the beaten path and rocky soil and devouring underbrush is all one sees. Some of the seed makes it to good ground and flowers into full harvest, and this is what justifies the whole process and is why one continues "to keep on keeping on" in any creative endeavor. Not everything we would like to do are we able to do because of factors beyond our control, but some good does come from our efforts; in fact, enough good that we do not "grow weary in well-doing," but faithfully stay with the process and keep at the task. This is the stance of authentic maturity, in my judgment, and one that can be hopefully applied to all the creative ventures in which one finds oneself involved. Be it a marriage, a business venture, whatever, the double aspect of this image of "playing one hand" should give helpful and liberating perspective.

On the one hand, it underlines the reality of one's limits, of the fact that many forces other than our own also impinge on the process and will affect the outcome. Therefore, neither excessive pride nor shame is appropriate in any endeavor. On the other hand, the image also underlines the real importance of human efforts. The fact that I do not do everything does not mean my efforts amount to nothing. The harvest in Jesus' parable was not as great as it would have been had all the seed come to flower, but had the sower given up altogether there would have been no harvest at all, and there was in fact a good one because he kept on sowing — ".250 hitter" though he turned out to be. This is precisely the balanced perspective that Jesus intended to set around the business of living, and while it can be applied helpfully to all of life's important ventures, let me focus on the sector of life that we have already celebrated; namely, the bringing of new life into the world and nurturing it into full humanness.

Accepting both sides of this image is utterly crucial. First, it really is true: We only play one hand in the game of those lives we touch. There are so many other factors at work. I saw some studies recently about the incredible impact that television is having on the average American today, and when you add that to the influence of peers and schools and other people in the family and community, it is very clear that what we do is important but it is only one of the things that go into the final formation of our personalities. This note really needs to be sounded both for the liberation and the encouragement of people in the process. For too long it seems there has been a tendency to define each other in the form of photocopying; that is, our success is measured by whether or not we turn out a carbon copy of ourselves as we help others along the way. This model is flawed from both a theoretical and a practical standpoint. It consists rather in recognizing the uniqueness of each individual and facilitating the emergence of that "only-one-of-its-kindness."

Our word "educate" comes from the Latin *educeo*, which means "to lead out" what has been placed within each of us by God's unrepeatable creativity. God does not mass-produce anything — even snowflakes or the tiniest daisy. To try to reproduce oneself exactly is literally "ungodly." The idea that we should or even have the right to make us over in another's image is theoretically wrong. Added to that is the practical problem — you do not really have the power to do so. Other forces impinge upon our life, and this not only has to be recognized in terms of humility, but can be celebrated in its positive implications. There is a joyful side to the realization that you only play one hand in the game of life. Think of all the other people who can bless and enrich us in ways that one person never could. That I only play one hand in the game is both a relief and occasion for celebration, and it would be nice if we could ponder this side of the image as a real gift of grace.

Yet the other side of the image is important as well. While you only play one hand, you do play a significant role, one not to be discounted or underestimated in any way. The delight we take in assisting others, that act of encouraging another, and then faithfully standing by them through thick and thin and passing on to them the truths you have learned about life are all highly significant. When this is done faithfully and consistently across the years, like the sower who continues to sow, its impact on the outcome and the whole culture will be felt.

I heard once of a mother of four little ones who finally got them to bed one evening and returned wearily to the den only to see an encyclopedia open on the floor with a page torn out of it. She went and got tape and stooped to repair the damage, and the act seemed to epitomize the whole of her life — forever picking up after children — and she wondered to herself, "Am I wasting my existence in pointless drudgery?" At the moment it seemed so. She pieced the torn fragments together and noticed they were the picture of a child's face. When she glued them back together, she happened to turn the pages over and there was a one page map of the whole world. And it dawned on her that as she was putting together correctly the countenance of a little child, she was also affecting the shape of the whole world. The old adage about "the hand that rocks the cradle rules the world" has much truth to it, and this side of "the one hand" image needs to be underlined as well as the other.

This brings me back to where we started. Jesus began his ministry in exuberance, and halfway through he told the parable of the soils. It represented his coming of age, I believe, coming to terms with both failure and potency, with the kind of creature he was and the kind of world in which we all live. Three out of four of his seeds did not make it, but some did. This is how he came to see life, and what kept him from blowing up or going down but keeping on. Listen, we only play one hand in the game of life, but the hand we do play matters! Wherever you are in some important endeavor this morning, be it marriage or parenting or a business venture, take this vision to heart. Let it become the frame of perspective you set around all your endeavors. It may humble you in relation to how you thought in the beginning, but rightly understood, it may enable you to finish and not give up too soon.

One hand, not everything to be sure, but something. Is it not time to start doing what we can with relish? I think so! What about you?

Proper 11
Pentecost 6
Ordinary Time 16
Matthew 13:24-30, 36-43

What You Don't Know Can Hurt You

He put before them another parable: "The kingdom of heaven may be compared to someone who sowed good seed in his field; but while everybody was asleep, an enemy came and sowed weeds among the wheat, and then went away. So when the plants came up and bore grain, then the weeds appeared as well. And the slaves of the householder came and said to him, 'Master, did you not sow good seed in your field? Where, then, did these weeds come from?' He answered, 'An enemy has done this.' The slaves said to him, 'Then do you want us to go and gather them?' But he replied, 'No; for in gathering the weeds you would uproot the wheat along with them. Let both of them grow together until the harvest; and at harvest time I will tell the reapers, collect the weeds first and bind them in bundles to be burned, but gather the wheat into my barn.' "...Then he left the crowds and went into the house. And his disciples approached him, saying, "Explain to us the parable of the weeds of the field." He answered, "The one who sows the good seed is the Son of Man; the field is the world, and the good seed are the children of the kingdom; the weeds are the children of the evil one, and the enemy who sowed them is the devil; the harvest is the end of the age, and the reapers are angels. Just as the weeds are collected and burned up with fire, so will it be at the end of the age. The Son of Man will send his angels, and they will collect out of his kingdom all causes of sin and all evildoers, and they will throw them into the furnace of fire, where there will be weeping and gnashing of teeth. Then the righteous will shine like the sun in the kingdom of their Father. Let anyone with ears listen!"

Each year, there is a Senior Recognition Sunday for our high school and college graduates. We do this because graduation is a significant milestone for all of us — not just for the graduates themselves, but also for their families and friends and all those who have contributed in some way to the educational processes of our community. The event of graduation can be described in many ways. For one thing, it is a *proud* time, for it represents the completion of a long and arduous process. No matter how one may have finished high school grade-wise, the fact that the person finished at all is no small achievement. Many have not done as much. Graduation is also a *sad* time, because for most people it signals the dissolving of certain clusters of relationships with family and friends who have been significant in the past. Graduation is also an *exciting* time, however, for it marks "a rite of passage," a freedom to explore opportunities and to show individuality. However, the aspect of graduation to think about and to emphasize in this sermon is not any of these, but is summed up in the adjective "dangerous." Why say that? Because it is easy in our culture to conclude that graduation marks the end of one's education and the need to learn. I am afraid we have a tendency to think of education as something you do in certain kinds of buildings at certain times of the day for a certain period of your life, and when that is over the learning phase of one's existence is complete. Nothing could be further from the truth. Maybe we can explore this assumption and make the point that *learning is for always*! At every stage in the human saga, it is imperative to keep educating ourselves and growing as best we can. We never get too old to learn and to expand. Stated in positive terms, the challenge is to maintain a learning stance toward life even though formal schoolroom days may be over. The same challenge, stated negatively, goes like this: "What you don't know most assuredly can hurt you."

The last statement is utterly true in the realm of factual knowledge and practical competence. The less you know about the basic realities of life, the greater difficulty you are going to have. A few years ago I attended a Rotary Club meeting and heard the speaker tell of a famous Mexican bank robber around the turn of the twentieth century named Jorge Rodriguez. It was his practice to slip over the border and raid a bank in Texas, then flee back into his native land. This became such a problem that the Texas Rangers assigned a whole posse to try to capture this bandit. One morning a Texas Ranger saw Jorge making his way into this country. He witnessed him robbing a bank and then stealthily followed him back over into Mexico to his hometown. As Jorge was relaxing in a cantina, the Texas Ranger slipped in, got the drop on him, and put his big .45 to his ear. Then he said to him loudly, "I know who you are, Jorge Rodriguez, and I know what you have been doing. Unless you give me back all the money you have taken from those Texas banks, I am going to blow your brains out." However, unfortunately, Jorge did not know a word of English and the Texas Ranger did not know Spanish, so there they were, two adults at a total impasse communicating. About that time, a little Mexican came up and said, "I know both languages, I'll translate for you," and proceeded to put the Ranger's proposal into language that Jorge could understand. He answered nervously, "Tell the big Texas Ranger that I want to live, that I haven't spent a single cent of that money. If he will go to the town, will face north, and count down seven stones, there will be a loose one. Pull it out and behind it he will find all the money I have taken. There are millions of dollars there untouched." With that, the little translator got a wry look on his face and turned to the Ranger and said, "Jorge Rodriguez is a brave man. He says he is ready to die." You see, "what you don't know can hurt you." Ask Jorge Rodriguez! Had he only learned a little English! Or the Texas Ranger — had he only learned a little Spanish. It was the one who did know that came out ahead.

I think it is important that we all come to terms with the fact that this is the way life works. There always has been and always will be a high premium placed on the competence that comes from knowing. It follows, therefore, that you cannot know too much about your chosen area of work or about the other realms of knowledge that impinge upon your existence. There is really no substitute for competence. No matter how intensely you may desire to do something or how much physical vitality you may possess, if you do not know the facts and therefore how to do a certain thing, you will be frustrated. Back when computers were first being used, a repairman was called out to a firm because their installation was malfunctioning. It took him about two minutes to size up the problem; he pushed a couple of keys and the computer began to work beautifully. Some days later the manager got a bill for $150 from this repairman, and he was incensed. He called the repairman and said: "You were not here over five minutes, and what you did anybody could have done. How do you justify such a charge?" The repairman replied: "The breakdown goes like this: $5 for pushing the keys, $145 for knowing which keys to push." I think this is an accurate assessment of the relative value of competence and power. It is true, any able-bodied person could have done that physical act. It was having knowledge of the product and how to assess the problem and what to do it with that was the valued factor.

Therefore, my thesis stated negatively is true in relation to factual knowledge and practical competence: "What you don't know in these realms can hurt you." Obviously no one possesses all the knowledge that is going to be called for out there in the long future. Only then does one realize that learning is for always, and educating yourself is something that rightly belongs to the whole of life, not just to the early morning hours. The question is, will we be able to meet this challenge?

This same dictum is also true in the realm of self-knowledge: "What you don't know about the inner workings of your own personhood can hurt you deeply." What I am saying is that we need to be on several different journeys simultaneously as we move through life. I have already spoken of "the outward journey," of extending your factual knowledge and practical competence. Now, I am suggesting "an inward journey," that disciplined effort to get in touch with our feelings, fears, hopes, and dreams; in a word, with that entire mysterious universe that exists deep within your being. There is much more going on inside of us than just of what we are conscious. This is the place where Sigmund Freud really has been helpful. He has made us all aware that there are unconscious forces at work within us all the time, and nothing is more important than getting increasingly in touch with these factors and learning how to utilize them.

In the parable from Matthew's gospel, Jesus tells of the enemy that came to sow weeds in the wheat field of a certain man. Karl Menninger, well-known American psychiatrist, discovered an ancient manuscript that contains an interesting sequel to Jesus' story. It reads: "And then the servants counseled together saying, 'It would be much better to pull out those weeds right now rather than wait, but we must obey the master, even when he is wrong. In the meantime, let us look about for the enemy who would do this evil thing to our master, who is kind to everyone and doesn't deserve this treatment.'" So they quietly inquired and searched in all the region round about, but they could find no one. One of the servants came privately to the chief steward at night, saying, "Sir, forgive me, but I can no longer bear to conceal my secret. I know the enemy who sowed the tares. I saw him do it." At this the chief steward was astonished and full of anger. But before punishing him, the steward demanded of the servant why he had not come forward sooner. "I dared not," cried the servant. "I scarcely dared to come and tell you this even now. I was awake the night the weeds were sown. I saw the man who did it; he walked past me, seemingly awake and yet asleep, and he did not appear to recognize me. But I recognized him." "And who was he, indeed?" asked the chief steward in great excitement. "Tell me, so that he can be punished." The servant hung his head. Finally, in a low voice he replied, "It was the master himself." And the two agreed to say nothing of this to any man. Now, the point is, of course, that at an unconscious level many of us are working at cross-purposes with our stated objectives. We are unwittingly sabotaging our own lives and acting in the grip of self-destructive forces of which we are not even aware. This is what makes imperative some kind of "inward journey," for unless we work to bring more of ourselves into the light of consciousness, we are destined to do what that man did — in that we need other people's reality-perception to add to our subjectivity, and this only comes by a "sleepwalk" of unconscious action, or we will sow tares in our own wheat fields.

Jesus was fully aware of the fact that what we do not know in terms of self-knowledge can hurt us. Do you remember that haunting prayer he uttered from the cross, so full of compassion and yet also so plaintive? "Father, forgive them, for they know not what they do." He realized that there was more than raw, deliberate evil at work in that situation. Many of those people were doing things that they did not really understand. They were caught up in forces that they had not taken the trouble to perceive and thus could not control. So much of the hurt that occurs on our human scene can be attributed to human blindness rather than to human badness. What we do not know about our unconscious forces and ourselves can most assuredly hurt us and other people.

Therefore, my second challenge is to never let up on "the inward journey." The kind of learning that needs to take place down in your depths is for always.

This dictum is also true in the third realm, and that is in relation to God. What you do not know about him will not only greatly diminish your joy but can also cripple and distort your whole life. I am speaking now about "the upward journey," and I realize that many people never even begin it because they have failed to learn the most basic single truth about God; namely, that he is a holy one. This word "holy" was not originally a moralistic term. It meant "separate," "unique," "only one of its kind." When applied to God, it means that he is a different sort of being than anything else we experience. There are actually just two orders of reality, the uncreated and the created. Everything in the world but God is in this second category — the created. Nothing else but God is in the first category. Now, what this means is that our experiences with God are going to be different than our experiences with anything else, and if you do not know that, you are destined to fail in "the upward journey." Many times people express these thoughts: "I've never seen God. God has never said anything to me. I can't taste or touch or feel God. Therefore, I don't believe there is such a reality." But such a statement is just like saying: "I can't smell the color red; therefore I don't believe such a thing as redness exists." Maybe what needs to be realized is that reality exists in many different forms, and we humans have been given a variety of capacities that relate to this diversity.

There is the reality of color, and corresponding to that is my capacity to smell. I can only get in touch with these realities when I use the appropriate perceiving mechanism that I have been given. All right, we humans also have a God-capacity, which is called "faith" in Holy Scripture, and it is something other than seeing, hearing, smelling, touching, or tasting. It is a way of knowing that may utilize any of these senses, yet it is distinct from them and beyond them all. The uncreated one has his own special way of making himself known to his creatures. Therefore, we should not expect our experiences of God to be the same as our experience with another human being or a rock or a flower. God is going to come to us in God's own way because God is the holy one — different, unique, and separate from every other created object. And the only way to begin to relate to God is to accept this fact and open ourselves to the kinds of onsets of mystery that are God's to give; it all depends if we are open enough to receive them. Thus, what some people do not know about God — namely, that God is different than anything else — hurts them in ever getting started on "the upward journey."

Which brings us back to where this all started. This time of year, as every year, congregations pause to acknowledge and commend those who have completed one part of their lives. It is many things: a proud time, a sad time, an exciting time, and also a dangerous time, dangerous if you make the mistake of thinking that your education is now over, that the time for learning is finished and that the challenge to grow is now behind you. This is not true! All of life, not just the beginning of life, is meant for learning. This is our challenge: Take the tools that we have been given and get on with the business of "the outward journey," of learning facts and practical competence; "the inward journey" of learning more and more about "all that is within you"; and "the upward journey" of learning all you can about God. Why? Because what you don't know in all these areas most assuredly can hurt you!

Proper 12
Pentecost 7
Ordinary Time 17
Matthew 13:31-33, 44-52

Face-to-Face With the Kingdom

He put before them another parable: "The kingdom of heaven is like a mustard seed that someone took and sowed in his field; it is the smallest of all the seeds, but when it has grown it is the greatest of shrubs and becomes a tree, so that the birds of the air come and make nests in its branches." He told them another parable: "The kingdom of heaven is like yeast that a woman took and mixed in with three measures of flour until all of it was leavened."... The kingdom of heaven is like treasure hidden in a field, which someone found and hid; then in his joy he goes and sells all that he has and buys that field. Again, the kingdom of heaven is like a merchant in search of fine pearls; on finding one pearl of great value, he went and sold all that he had and bought it. Again, the kingdom of heaven is like a net that was thrown into the sea and caught fish of every kind; when it was full, they drew it ashore, sat down, and put the good into baskets but threw out the bad. So it will be at the end of the age. The angels will come out and separate the evil from the righteous and throw them into the furnace of fire, where there will be weeping and gnashing of teeth. "Have you understood all this?" They answered, "Yes." And he said to them, "Therefore every scribe who has been trained for the kingdom of heaven is like the master of a household who brings out of his treasure what is new and what is old."

Several years ago I came to one of those "moments of truth" in my life that enabled me to see more deeply into myself and into the challenge of the Christian gospel. Interestingly enough, the issue at stake was my emotional attitude toward the weather. In order to appreciate this situation, you need to realize that all my life I have had a special affection for snow. Of all the seasons of the year winter is my favorite, and the part of winter that I like best is the coming of that "icy white stuff." As long as I can remember, I have loved to see it fall, delighted to walk in it and slide on it, and to my wife's dismay I do not even mind driving in it! I am never happier weather-wise than when a big snow is either on the way or has already arrived. For reasons I cannot explain I simply came into this world with an emotional bias in favor of snow, and for years this predilection colored the feeling of my whole existence from November until May. I would watch weather forecasts with the emotional involvement of a partisan sports fan. If snow were predicted for the next few hours, I would swell with anticipation and go to bed exuberant. If, however, clear sunshine were the prospect, I felt like turning off the forecaster and would go to bed depressed.

Now, you may wonder what this account of my belated coming-of-age emotionally has to do with the sermon topic, but believe me, there is a connection! You see, there is a profound kinship between the words "the kingdom of heaven is like..." and my reactions several years ago in relation to the weather. The parables of Matthew 13 represent a way in which we as humans can relate to something that is larger than our world of reality. It is a way that we can look at things we understand: a mustard seed, yeast, a pearl of great price, a fishing net. These represent ways we can understand not only how the kingdom works but how valuable it is. The parable stories help us resolve "to take the trip of life by bus and leave the driving to God," moving from an essentially egocentric approach toward life to acknowledging and accepting the other realities of life. It is getting the relation of the creature and the Creator into their proper sequence as far as structuring reality is concerned. It is deciding who does the acting and who does the reacting in life, or put another way, how human desire and historical reality are to be related to each other.

There are obviously more messages in these parables; however, Jesus seems to be trying to get people to see what is right in front of them. Parables have a way of moving us into a room to look at the photos on the wall, only to have the door shut behind us and see the photos are of each of us. The first two parables of our lection have to do with growth. In the first, the mustard seed grows from a tiny seed to a large shrub or tree. The second also represents growth, but a growth of yeast as it almost secretly goes throughout the dough. These two parables seem to be letting us in on something about the kingdom that we do not always see. It is easy to talk about a kingdom as being something out there or other, but in this case the kingdom of heaven is something that grows around and within us. Citizenship in this kingdom is not something that we actually make happen for ourselves. It is something that God does for us. There has been much debate over the years about the 14th Amendment to the U.S. Constitution, which gives everyone born or naturalized in this country citizenship. This amendment comes from the English lordship idea of a king and those who live in his domain. If you are born into the domain you are part of the kingdom. It is much like what happens with us when we become citizens of God's kingdom.

How do we as people that live in this world and relate to this world come to a point where we look at the spiritual realm as a kingdom for us? Maybe there are a couple ways of looking at this. One possibility is to do what we do so naturally, to make individual desire the beginning point and attempt to deal with reality on this basis. This is a way of making the kingdom of heaven fit into our set of ideas or concepts. This approach leads to satisfaction for us, for there are times when reality does assume the shape of one's desire — snow does on occasion come — and then you are happy. But far more often this is not the case. What you face is that which you do not like — all that sun in January — and, try as you will, there is nothing you can do but become more frustrated. For you see, when a finite creature with only a limited amount of power tries to get into the business of structuring reality, this can only lead to anguish. It is assuming a role in life that is utterly beyond one's capacities. However, regardless of our desire to make the kingdom in our own image, it would be a complete undoing of the kingdom to fit what we think would be good. Since God is God and I am not, this approach is certainly not an avenue that Jesus would embrace or accept.

Another approach to the kingdom is to try to see all the good people in the world and then pattern our lives after those people. The problem with this is that we can always find the flaws in any person. The solution to the kingdom approach is what Jesus did in Matthew 13. He told parables that would allow a person to view the kingdom in a way that would give us a sense of what the kingdom does and how it spreads. Not only that he emphasized how important this line of kingdom thinking is, and therefore told these stories about finding great treasure or a pearl of great price. This is the approach of accepting what God has done and then letting our feelings move us to seek and discover within what God has put as desirable, rather than wanting everything to be different.

This means walking out in the morning and starting with whatever is there and looking for what is good in it and celebrating that without wanting something else. I found after long experience that this was a far more productive way for a creature like me to cope with the realities of life, and this I believe is exactly what Jesus was calling for when he taught us "the kingdom of God is like..." because it represents the way a human being ought to feel when he finally "comes to himself" and come to recognize his true place in the universe. After all, we are finite creatures with not just limited power but with very limited vision and perspective on reality as well. No one of us is really good enough or wise enough or strong enough to know how to structure reality for the good of the whole universe. Think of the mess the world would get into if each one of us got to have his own way as far as the weather were concerned. What an erratic jumble it would be!

However, according to the Bible, God is not what we are. God is bigger and wiser and better than any of us, and structuring reality for the good of all is something God can do. Thus, coming to recognize these twin facts — our insufficiency to be creators and God's adequacy for this role — are what lie behind the statement "The kingdom of God is like..." All through the gospels Jesus speaks of this kingdom as something positive, attractive, and appealing. He compares it to a treasure one finds in a field or a pearl that is obviously of great value. The moment a person discovers this sort of thing, he naturally begins to want it above all else.

But how do we develop such positive feelings about the kingdom of God? What has to happen to us so that we realize that the rule of God is infinitely superior to any form of words, how do we come to the place where we can desire a kingdom that is worth everything in the world or realize that it is spreading silently? As we ponder the process of how the kingdom comes to be positively desired, maybe we can see it happening in two ways.

Some people come to this by the position route; that is, early on in life they somehow sense that God is the highest God and realize that what God has to give is infinitely superior to anything they could create. Thus they accept life, and know that even when it is not what we would like it to be it is not ours to have control over. Otherwise we would be in a state of profound dissatisfaction and alienation. It would be as it is for those who do not like anything about the gift of life as it is being given — and do not like themselves or their parents or their place in history or anything — they want it all changed and waste no time and effort in setting about to do this. For example, at the beginning of the parable of the prodigal son there is a classic example of a person who makes individual desire the beginning point and proceeds to deal with reality accordingly. This person is not pleased with anything they see, and sets out to reorder the world in the likeness of their wishes. When we do not take anything else into account as we proceed to do this — the feelings of family, the future of business — nothing matters except getting to where we want to go and doing what we want to do. In that parable, as you know, this person got his chance — inheritance, the far country freedom, and all — and soon it became apparent that he was ill-equipped to be the creator of a universe. His desires were so small and selfish and unwise that when he acted upon them, nothing creative resulted. The process was one of unmaking and disintegration rather than creating and building up. This happened to the boy. It was his "moment of truth," like mine long ago.

The Greek term is that "he came to himself." It is a medical image for recovering from a coma or waking up out of a swoon. What happened was that the prodigal suddenly realized who he was and what he was not in this universe. He had learned by virtue of his pain what he had refused to be taught in any other way. It suddenly became clear to him that as a finite creature he was not good enough or wise enough or strong enough to structure a universe. His personal desires were not adequate to be the basis of reality. And it was at that point that the memory of his father and the way he approached life began to look very differently to the young man. At that moment the wisdom and goodness and power of "one who was better than he" became very attractive, and he resolved to move toward that one and relate to him in a positive way. This "coming to himself" and deciding "to go to his father" is a good picture of what is involved in the words "the kingdom of God is like," for they represent the admission that we are but finite creatures, not creators, that we are not good enough or wise enough or powerful enough to structure life on our own terms, and that we do need to submit ourselves to another who knows more about reality than we do. Our place on the bus of life as humans is not in the driver's seat but in the back, where we can participate in what another, who is better and bigger and wiser than we, knows how to give.

What a contrast there is between what the prodigal did in attempting to create and what God did with the same process. According to the faith story of Genesis, the almighty is adequate for such a task, for look at how God did it in the beginning with such adequacy and skill. The idea to create was God's own. It was not forced upon God or squeezed out of God by another. God decided one day that the joy of aliveness was too good a thing to keep to God's self, so God resolved to create in order to share and enlarge the circle. Once having established a goal, God set about to fulfill it with grace and ease. There are no signs of struggle in Genesis. Then when God was done, the writer of this faith story says, God looked back on what was created and was pleased with what he had accomplished. "It is good, it is good, it is very, very good" was the ecstatic evaluation.

This whole account conveys the feeling that here is a Creator who knows what is going on. What a contrast this is to the prodigal's experience. When he got an idea and set out to act upon it, he neither knew what to do or how to do it, nor was he pleased at the finish with what he had done. As a creator of reality, the prodigal son was "a bust"; he was "out of his league." He was attempting to do something he was neither good enough nor wise enough nor strong enough to do. But it was only on the far side of failure that he finally learned his lesson, and the sad truth is: this is where most of us have to go before we "come to ourselves" and learn the stories of the kingdom, how it works, and how valuable it is.

Here, then, is the issue at stake — the decision of a finite creature to be just that — a finite creature — and for the ultimate Creator to be the Creator. You can arrive at the decision from one of two directions — by realizing somehow that God is God and God is good and gladly deciding "to take the trip of life by bus and leave the driving to him," or by suffering… by "having a go" at attempting to build the world according to our desires, and like the prodigal, seeing what comes of it. Either way, the conclusion is the same — we finite creatures with our desires for snow or adventure or freedom or whatever is neither good enough nor wise enough or strong enough to structure reality as a whole, but God is!

As the ancient mystics put it: "God is our peace, our beginning, our ending, our only source of joy." When we hear these parables again for the first time, it is my prayer that we see more clearly what it is like when we realize "the kingdom of heaven is like…" May God hasten the day that this happens to us all!

Proper 13
Pentecost 8
Ordinary Time 18
Matthew 14:13-21

Gratitude and Coping

Now when Jesus heard this, he withdrew from there in a boat to a deserted place by himself. But when the crowds heard it, they followed him on foot from the towns. When he went ashore, he saw a great crowd; and he had compassion for them and cured their sick. When it was evening, the disciples came to him and said, "This is a deserted place, and the hour is now late; send the crowds away so that they may go into the villages and buy food for themselves." Jesus said to them, "They need not go away; you give them something to eat." They replied, "We have nothing here but five loaves and two fish." And he said, "Bring them here to me." Then he ordered the crowds to sit down on the grass. Taking the five loaves and the two fish, he looked up to heaven, and blessed and broke the loaves, and gave them to the disciples, and the disciples gave them to the crowds. And all ate and were filled; and they took up what was left over of the broken pieces, twelve baskets full. And those who ate were about five thousand men, besides women and children.

Nothing in recent years has been more upsetting than the sharp increase in the use of drugs among young. People have become so traumatized by the subject that any reasonable discussion of it has become well-nigh impossible. This is why I was particularly impressed with a speech made not long ago by a public health official at a large university, for he wisely avoided histrionics and went straight to the heart of the problem. He openly acknowledged that "the jury was still out" as to all of the physical effects that might result from using drugs, illegal and legal. At this point we simply do not know the full impact these drugs may have on our physical organism, and he urgently called for more and better research in this area. However, he went on to say at another point that "the jury was already back in" about the psychological effects of such a habit upon personality structure. He noted that learning to cope with difficulty and stress is one of life's most basic challenges. The pattern one develops at this point early in life goes a long way toward the shaping of one's personhood, and this is why the use of hallucinatory drugs can be so damaging. In a word, they offer an escape from reality. This is not a new idea, but really another form of something very old; namely, the practice of running away from "things-as-they-are" into a region of contrived fantasy. The speaker underlined the fact that psychologically this could be the most damaging aspect of drug usage, for while we are still learning what it does to our physical cells, we do know something of what it does to the human spirit — it encourages the strategy of escapism as a way of coping with difficulty. If this be true, then long after the use of the drugs themselves may be discontinued "a melody may linger on," and it could be an infinitely sad one, for escapism as a way of doing life is tragically inadequate, and if one persists down this road long enough it can only lead to deeper emptiness.

I found this to be a very wise word on a troubled subject. However, it raises the deeper question: namely, how does one cope in a healthy way with the stresses of life? It is important to be informed as to what will not work in this area, but it is even more important to be given some positive model of coping that will enable us to face up to things as they are and deal with them creatively rather than running away. And the question becomes: Where can such a positive model be found?

I would like to affirm that there is such a model in the figure of Jesus of Nazareth. Here is one who is far ahead of us in terms of knowing "how to put it all together." Again and again in the pages of the New Testament he can be seen coping directly and courageously with all kinds of difficulties, and in the passage from Matthew there is one of those episodes for us to view how he dealt with situations in his life and also learn what we can from it. This is one of the best-known events of his entire ministry — the time he fed the 5,000 in the wilderness. This episode must have made a deep impression on his disciples, for it is the only miracle in the whole ministry of Jesus that all four of the gospels record. I imagine the outline of the story is already familiar to most of us, but you may be surprised at just how relevant it turns out to be as a model for coping with difficulty. Here was our Lord up against a gigantic problem. The way he responded is worthy of most careful attention.

Perhaps a word about the background of this event will set the whole picture in clearer perspective. At this particular moment, Jesus and his disciples were trying to get away by themselves so that they could reflect on the mission that the twelve had just completed. Galilee was a crowded, densely populated place by the Sea of Galilee to the more sparsely inhabited eastern shore. However, the crowds saw Jesus and his disciples in their boats and ran all the way around the northern end of the sea so that when Jesus and his disciples pulled onto land, they would be facing the same pleading multitudes. One of the incredible things about Jesus was that he never regarded needy human beings as a nuisance. Rather, out of great compassion he rearranged his plans and worked with the folks for the rest of the day. However, his disciples were hardly as flexible or as generous in their attitudes, and by late afternoon they "had had it up to here" with this crowd and wanted to get rid of them. Besides, they realized the people were getting hungry and tired, and that crowds in this condition can often grow hostile and get out of hand. So they pulled Jesus aside and pointed out to him the crisis that was in the making and strongly suggested that he disperse the people before things went from bad to worse. It was a perfectly natural suggestion to make in the face of the situation. Here was a problem the disciples wanted to get away from, and it seemed to them that the best strategy was to disengage and let someone else worry about the hunger and the tempers of the crowd. "Send them away" was their advice to Jesus. "Let them go into the villages and countryside to solve their hunger problem." But Jesus saw things differently. His way of coping involved three significant steps.

First, he rejected the strategy of escapism and chose rather to face up to the problem squarely and openly. Instead of saying, "Let's get rid of these difficult people," he said, "We are involved in this event. In fact, I am partly responsible for their being here so late, because I have been teaching and healing them. This is not a buck we have a right to pass. We must do something about this problem of hunger and the late hour. You give them something to eat." It is clear from this response that for Jesus the way out was always the way through. To him the solution of a problem never lay behind him or off on a tangent somewhere. It lay straight on the other side of the difficulty. For Jesus, the good news always comes by facing up to the bad news. Initially, then, Jesus chose to confront the difficulty head-on rather than seek a way of escape.

The second thing Jesus did was to identify the resources that were inherent in the situation. He caught the disciples by surprise by asking them to do something that had never occurred to them in their panic; namely, to find out what they had going for them amid all that seemed to be going against them. "How much food do we have?" was his pointed inquiry. It was actually a most reasonable question to ask, and the disciples were amazed to discover that, although there was not much, some food was available in the group — five loaves and two fish, to be exact.

The third and climactic step in the process came when Jesus took the available resources in his hands, lifted up his eyes to heaven in thanksgiving to God, and then without anxiety or panic set about the task of meeting the hunger of the crowd. It sounds so simple to say that he began to do something — the best he could with what he had — and yet that was the hinge on which the whole process turned, and you know as well as I do what happened as a result. Somehow, with God's help, that little became enough! What had seemed so impossible to the disciples as they looked exclusively at the problem, became a possibility through the decisive action of Jesus. He was not immobilized by the seeming disproportion of the need and the resources at hand. After all, beginnings, by their very nature, are always insignificant, and even the longest journey has to start with just one step. To the amazement of everybody present, Jesus began to act — gratefully and decisively — on the basis of what he had, and lo and behold, his action gathered strength from all directions, and turned what seemed like an insoluble problem into a great triumph.

Now, how are we to regard an event of this kind? Is what happened here so utterly miraculous that we are to feel no commonality with it or assume that only a divine being could do this sort of thing? I realize that this is the way many people look at this event, and thus dismiss it as having no practical application to their lives. But it seems this would be a bad mistake. After all, the church fathers used to say: "He became what we are that we might become what he is." Jesus did not come to earth to taunt us with his divinity or to make us feel inferior. He came to show us what a human being made in the image of God really could do. He not only opened our eyes to the vastness of God's nature, he also opened our eyes to the vastness of human nature. Did he not say to his disciples: "Greater works than I have done, you shall do"? His way of doing life and collaborating with God is a way that is open to us. Therefore, I will argue that this event can be taken as a concrete model of how any one of us can cope with the difficulties that we face. The way he did it is the way we can do it, if we only believed more fully in the vision of God to earth.

What I am saying is that the difference between my way of coping with difficulty and his is one of attitude, not capacity. For example, it is evident here that Jesus has come to terms with the fact that life is a process of problem-solving, pure and simple. He seems to have laid aside all those childish fantasies about there being a place where there is no conflict or difficulty or hardship. He accepts the fact that such a realm simply does not exist for us humans, and therefore he was free to focus all his energies on the challenges of existence, rather than dissipating them in trying to escape the inescapable or lamenting the way things are. This is so different from our tendencies in this area. Regardless of our age, we still have trouble coming to terms with the fact that life is problem-solving and problem-solving is life. We keep dreaming of some childlike paradise where all will be done for us and conflict and hassle simply do not exist. There is no way to total up the energy we have wasted looking for an easy way out, lamenting things rather than realistically coping.

I remember a story of a small boy who came down with a terrible cold, and somehow got it into his mind the idea that if he would run swiftly from one room to another, perhaps he could get away from those germs the way we could get away from my fat little puppy. It was his mother who discovered him darting from room to room all out of breath, and when she found out what he was attempting to do, she wisely and gently called him to reality. She explained that there was no special cure for colds, and no matter how fast a person runs or where that person goes, the germs go along. "The sooner you quit trying to run away from them and start taking medicine for it, the quicker you will get well," she said.

There is great truth here, not only about how to treat colds, but for all of life's problems. Yet humans have been slow in learning this. Coming to terms with the fact that life is problem-solving and that problem-solving is life has been difficult indeed, and yet this is the attitude that Jesus assumed. The truth is, we could grow up like that too, if we would. We do not have to go on forever looking for a "bed of roses," or remain in a childish world of fantasy and escapism. Jesus grew in "wisdom and in stature," and the truth is, so could I, if I would.

Another difference in attitude between Jesus' way of coping and my own was his recognition that resources are always present in problem situations. I must admit that in the face of stress, I am usually like the disciples were that day — the vastness of the difficulty so dominates my attention that I never think of looking on the resource side. Fear has a way of making us shortsighted and reducing our field of vision, and in the face of problems we have been totally one-sided in our outlook. However, as Jesus demonstrated here, such a way of looking at things is simply not realistic. It denies the presence of God in all that God has created and makes God out as some remote, absentee landlord who is only present at the beginning and the end of life. All through his ministry Jesus opposed this "absentee" concept of God. While he certainly was open to the possibility of the miraculous, he also affirmed God's active presence in what already existed.

For example, during his temptation experience, the tempter suggested to Jesus that the only way to meet his need for food was to have God "intervene" and make bread out of stone, implying that the only help to be found was outside the situation. Jesus wisely rejected this temptation and chose rather to rely on the power of God that was already inherent in the seed and the earth and the process of growth. He said in effect: "I choose to utilize what God has already placed here, rather than relying on intervention." What a blindness to reality it is to imagine any situation without some positive resources. There are always "five loaves and two fish" in the midst of our problems, if only we have the eyes to see, and of course, Jesus had such eyes. And the point is, we could see too, if we would let Jesus teach us how to open our eyes. Once again, the difference between Jesus and us is one of attitude and developing a potential that is present already.

A third difference in Jesus' way and pattern lies in his resolve to begin to act in terms of what he had, rather than being immobilized by a problem. Being immobilized by a problem is a common approach that we usually take, and nothing increases anxiety more than inactivity. The longer we stand motionless before a problem, the worse it gets. By the same token, the very decision to act, no matter how partial it may seem, will often break the spell and turn the tide. In a little country inn in England there is a carving over the fireplace with this saying: "Fear knocked at the door. Faith answered, and no one was there." This is so true of every stress-filled situation. What one finds is that facing up is often not as fearful as what you expect when you are tempted to back down. The ability to start acting, then, even when it seems partial, is an utterly crucial step in any problem-solving, and once again Jesus was able to do this. He took the five loaves and two fish in hand and began to do something. And so could we, if by his help we would let him teach us to act.

The point I am laboring to make is that Jesus' way of coping, radical as it may seem in comparison to our ways, is not an utterly impossible pattern. The things he did that day in the face of an enormous problem are things that any one of us could do if we would allow him to teach us. You see, the capacity to accept problems for what they are, to look for resources that are already there, and to begin to act with God's help on the basis of what we have are all within our potential as made in the image of God.

The question becomes: How was Jesus able to so cope and find the courage to face problems and see resources and begin to act? I think the secret of it all is found in something to which I have already alluded, and this is the stance of gratitude in which Jesus received all of life. Each one of the gospels tells us that while everyone else was murmuring and wringing their hands, Jesus calmly looked up to heaven and gave thanks to God for what he had. This was the stance out of which Jesus lived his whole life, and right here is the profound secret of his coping. He believed two things, and those were that God is good — really and truly for us and not against us — and that God is involved dynamically in all the events of our lives. That is not to say we humans are puppets and everything that occurs is directly the result of God's will. There are many centers of power in history since humans are free. However, "in all things," says Saint Paul, "God is at work for good," which means that every event has some positive potential and in that sense is a gift to be received and unwrapped.

It is amazing how differently things begin to look when gratitude becomes the basic stance. A stance of gratitude also opens our eyes to the resources that do exist in the midst of our problems and keeps us from ever saying, "There is nothing here that can be used." No matter how deep the crisis, God has not left any situation without its "five loaves and two fish," and gratitude is the way to have our eyes opened to what is already present. Such gratitude also encourages one to begin with what he has and to expect more to rise to meet him as he moves. After all, what one has at the beginning has been given him by a gracious God. Can he not then be expected to give more as the task unfolds? This is what Jesus did. He began to act out of profound stance of gratefulness, and such a beginning gathered strength from heaven and earth and the multitude was fed.

Coming back then to a most crucial question: How can we learn to cope with the difficulties that we encounter? There are a thousand unhealthy ways of coping — drugs being one of them. However, I know at least one infinitely healthy way, and that is what Jesus can be seen doing in the wilderness. There in the shadow of great difficulty, he faced up rather than ran away. He laid hold of the resources already present in the situation rather than expecting intervention. He began to act in terms of what he had, and it worked — infinitely and beautifully. And the truth is: We can do the same thing in relation to our problems. How? By letting Jesus show us the Father, reconciling us to the fact that God who gives us our life is good, and thus enabling us to receive the events of life in gratitude rather than resentment. When this is our stance, the courage to cope will rise up from the depths. The problems? They will assume the shape of challenges. The difficulties? They will be seen as the bearers of hidden resources. The crises? They will become the moments to begin. Here, then, is the way to cope. May God give us the grace, here as everywhere, to follow the man of gratitude!

Proper 14
Pentecost 9
Ordinary Time 19
Matthew 14:22-33

Giving and Receiving

Immediately he made the disciples get into the boat and go on ahead to the other side, while he dismissed the crowds. And after he had dismissed the crowds, he went up the mountain by himself to pray. When evening came, he was there alone, but by this time the boat, battered by the waves, was far from the land, for the wind was against them. And early in the morning he came walking toward them on the sea. But when the disciples saw him walking on the sea, they were terrified, saying, "It is a ghost!" And they cried out in fear. But immediately Jesus spoke to them and said, "Take heart, it is I; do not be afraid." Peter answered him, "Lord, if it is you, command me to come to you on the water." He said, "Come." So Peter got out of the boat, started walking on the water, and came toward Jesus. But when he noticed the strong wind, he became frightened, and beginning to sink, he cried out, "Lord, save me!" Jesus immediately reached out his hand and caught him, saying to him, "You of little faith, why did you doubt?" When they got into the boat, the wind ceased. And those in the boat worshiped him, saying, "Truly you are the Son of God."

A wise person, according to Sam Keen, the author of *Fire in the Belly*, is one who knows what time it is in his or her life; that is, they have a sense of the appropriate which enables them to know what to do amid a baffling array of options. Keen tells of going one summer to visit relatives who lived in the tidewater area of Virginia, where there are many little bays adjoining the Atlantic Ocean. Some of the old-timers there warned him about the peculiar dangers of swimming in that area, particularly at those times of the day when the tide was coming in or going out. They advised him that if he found himself caught in either of those periods of turbulence, the thing to do was not to try to swim against the current, for that would be impossible, but rather simply to float and allow the tide to carry him either in or out of the bay. There the waters would quiet down and it would be relatively easy to swim across to the shore. People who did not understand this strategy, however, often times were frightened and in trying to swim their way out had drowned. The secret of negotiating those tricky waters, therefore, involved three essential skills — the ability to float (this may also let us think about how to receive a floating device), the ability to swim, and most important of all, the wisdom to know when to do the one and then the other.

I wonder if Peter thought about any of the survival tricks he had learned as a fisherman that would lend themselves to accepting the invitation of Jesus as we approach this well-known story of Jesus walking on the water and Peter's desire to walk to him?

This story certainly gets our imagination going, when Jesus decided to demonstrate his supernatural ability to walk on water. It wasn't survival that Peter was thinking about when he asked if he could walk to Jesus. We often speak of the lack of faith Peter had; however, to me it showed remarkable faith for Peter to step from the boat onto the water with no survival strategy in mind. It gets me to think why this story was told and retold, and why it was added to the gospel accounts.

We live in a society that looks for security on every hand and how we can negotiate the waters around us and how if possible we would have a survival plan if something goes wrong. This scripture speaks to the reality of "troubled waters," and how our dependence on Jesus will take away some of the fear and anxiety.

I try to put myself into the place in which scripture is speaking and I constantly ask people when they read scripture: "Whom do you stand with in this passage?" It is always easy to stand with Jesus, since he always has things right; however, most of our lives are not lived in the Jesus world but rather in the world of Peter or one of the other disciples. Maybe I can stand with the disciples left in the boat. They are afraid and seem helpless, and Jesus knew they would welcome help from forces other than themselves; specifically, letting things around them happen that they have no control over, and letting other people do things for them and with them that they cannot do for themselves.

Or maybe with the advice of the "old-timers" from the Atlantic seaboard and the ability to swim. I am sure that Peter, being a fisherman, had the ability to swim, but his ability does not show up in this story. He seems to be a symbol for the willingness to act energetically and make a difference by the deliberate insertion of our energies into a given situation. We always question Peter's good sense to know when to do what — that stands for the ability to recognize what time it really is, and thus know what is appropriate to do or let be done in a given moment.

My hunch is that all of us need a little bit of Peter in ourselves to step out into the unknown and walk to the one calling us. I do not know anyone who is perfectly developed in all of these areas, and one of the creative uses to which we can put this crisis is right at this point — we can allow it to teach us something about ourselves and where we need to do some growth — work in our journey toward becoming more functioning human beings. This challenge, of course, will vary from individual to individual, depending on where you are in your own development.

For example, the greatest challenge facing many folk just now — particularly those who live in different parts of the world — will be learning how to float or use a floatation device. When Peter begins to sink, his floating device (or should I say his saving device) was Jesus himself. One of the hardest things we do is letting others help us, regardless of how deep the water is, or being helped and receiving from others without shame or guilt, in the process discovering a whole new form of human satisfaction. This is no easy task for the person who has become accustomed to being strong and helping other people rather than being helped. For those who have always imagined themselves and maybe even prided themselves on being self-reliant and the givers of charity rather than the recipient of charity, it is quite a switch to find the roles suddenly reversed — but this is precisely what happens when crises descend and suddenly the world is literally "turned upside down."

My point is that some needed growth can take place in a situation such as this, for the truth is, none of us can be "strong" all the time. The notion of total self-reliance is an illusion, because all human beings are creatures by nature, which means we depend or "hang," as the root of that term implies, on forces other than ourselves. I heard once of the self-made man who said that if he had it to do all over again, he would call in some help. Of course, the deeper truth is that he had lots of help all along and simply did not recognize it. One of the great things this whole trauma can do for us is to teach us just how limited and dependent we really are, and call us to a greater sense of humility and interrelatedness than ever before. We do need others if we are going to survive in our kind of world, and the willingness to receive help and be acted upon is an utterly crucial capacity, but many folk have some real growing to do in order to come to terms with this fact and incorporate it into their image of themselves.

The book of James says that often "you have not because you ask not," and I have seen this happen again and again during different crises. I recall once seeing volunteers asking a woman if she needed any more help in trying to get what possessions she could. The woman answered instinctively, "No, thank you. We have all the help we need." The truth was they could have used four or five more men but now it was too late.

Here was a case of not really knowing when to reach out and use the saving device, to use my earlier symbol. Here were wealthy, self-reliant folk who were highly developed in the art of giving help to others, but under-developed in those other two survival skills — knowing how to receive help and recognizing what time it actually was at that given moment. Folk like this may even be the victims of excessive Christian idealism. This principle applies to that saying of Jesus that we have had ground in us from our youth on: "It is more blessed to give than to receive." There is an obvious and powerful element of truth in these words, but they can be pushed too far if they are taken to mean that one must always give and never under any circumstances receive. There is a blessedness in knowing how to be helped that is in fact different from the blessedness of helping, but it is nonetheless real and significant and learning this lesson may be one of the most important challenges facing many people.

The old-timers in Virginia warned Sam Keen that it was the really good swimmers who often got into the most trouble, because they thought their one skill was enough by itself, when it was not. It may have even been so with Peter since he had been in all kinds of seas and when he asked to "come to Jesus" he stepped outside the boat. I am not sure if that was all faith on Peter's part or if there was some self-reliance. I think it is easy to look around us when we are on our faith journey and take our eyes away from Jesus and become the one sinking instead of the one walking. The same is true of those who have been self-reliant all their days — the givers of help rather than the recipients of help. These types may be in the gravest danger. It takes three skills to survive the kind of turbulence we are in, not just one. Learning how to receive the help needed and recognizing when this is appropriate is a high order of the day, but not the only challenge to be sure.

Others in communities everywhere may need to learn how to use their own faith more vigorously. If the crisis that "turned the world upside down" left some who had been strong in a position of need, it also catapulted some who had always thought of themselves as weak into a position of power. If too much of any good thing becomes a bad thing, it is equally true that too little of a good thing is also bad. One of the hopes I have for our world in the days ahead is that not only will we "learn to stay in the boat," but also that we will "learn to walk on the water," which is simply another way of saying that all of us need to experience growth in those places where we are underdeveloped and thus move toward the fully functioning human condition that is God's will for all of us.

After all, was not this the real objective of Jesus' ministry, which shows us in microcosm what God is trying to accomplish in his world? Jesus attempted to do two things basically in the days of his flesh — he humbled the proud, making those who thought only of their power aware also of their needs; and he exalted the downtrodden, that is, he made those who had imaged themselves as powerless aware of their worth and potency. In this sense he was a revolutionary of the highest order, and unless I am badly mistaken he is still trying to do the same two things among us today, this crisis is simply a golden opportunity to see the issues more vividly and get on with the particular kind of growing that is called for given one's individual situation.

The best thing about this "walking on the water" story is our model in Jesus and the help he offered to the disciples, for what Jesus tried to effect in others he lived out authentically in his life. You see, better than any other person who has ever lived on this earth, Jesus knew how to swim, use his ability to float, use help from others, and use their wisdom when it was appropriate. Again and again in the pages of the gospel of Matthew, you see him giving himself unstintingly that others might be helped. The scripture lesson gives us a little insight into one of the most exciting and unusual stories in all the Bible. This miracle of stilling the waters and saving Peter lets us sit with the disciples and walk with Peter in a dangerous and scary world. Jesus was moved again and again to teach his disciples of faith and dependence, and that gives us all a view of the mission of our Lord then and today.

He knew what it was to suffer, and he also knew the gift of receiving the blessing of life and living it. The other part of the scripture lesson reflects the time that he made everything calm and not just a place in the storm. He sensed the spirit of the disciples as they came to believe more and more about living and believing in Jesus: "Truly you are the Son of God." To many it is much easier to turn to God when the storm or crisis is around, but what happens to us when the seas calm down? The storms as shown in this story, come when least expected, and our response must be to both the storm and the calm.

Jesus knew how to receive and how to let other people do things for him. He knew how to swim, taking care of himself, and he knew how to float or use those things from others. He developed the wisdom to recognize what time it was — that sense of the appropriate that enabled him to know when to do what. In my judgment, one of the great challenges of this moment is right at this point — to use a crisis "to gain a heart of wisdom," as the Psalmist puts it, to learn where we are and how we need to grow.

You and you alone can determine the particular shape the challenge assesses for you. It may be to learn how to float — master the art of receiving and being helped and the joy of gratitude that comes with that. Or it may be learning to swim — assuming your part of the load at last and learning the joy of creativity and helping. Or it may be the acquiring of wisdom — discerning what time it really is and learning when to do what. But whichever, please do not let this experience be wasted. We have lost too much else not to gain something in the process.

If You Like This Book...

Rev. Dr. Tom Garrison has also written sections of "Building a Victorious Life" a part of the Pentecost (Middle Third) section of *Sermons on the Gospel Readings*, Series II, Cycle C (978-0-7880-2399-6) (printed book $40.95, e-book $29.95); and *A Call to Love*, Pentecost (Middle Third), Cycle A (978-0-7880-1830-5) (printed book $8.95, e-book $6.95).

contact
CSS Publishing Company, Inc.
www.csspub.com
800-241-4056
orders@csspub.com

Prices are subject to change without notice.

www.ingramcontent.com/pod-product-compliance
Lightning Source LLC
Chambersburg PA
CBHW071739040426
42446CB00012B/2400